**Portrait of Alfred Russel Wallace,
J.W.Beaufort,
Natural History Museum**

From a look at a globe or a map of the eastern hemisphere, we shall perceive between Asia and Australia several large and small islands, forming a connected group distinct from those great masses of land, and having little connection with either of them. Situated upon the equator, and bathed by the tepid water of the great tropical oceans, this region enjoys a climate more uniformly hot and moist than any other part of the globe, and teems with natural productions which are elsewhere unknown. The richest of fruits and the most precious of spices are indigenous here. It produces the giant flowers of the Rafflesia, the great green-winged Ornithoptera (princes among butterfly tribes), the man-like orang-utan and the gorgeous birds of paradise.

It is inhabited by a peculiar and interesting race of mankind - the Malay, found nowhere beyond the limits of this insular tract, which has been named the Malay Archipelago.

THE WALLACE LINE

IAN BURNET

Alfred Street Press

THE WALLACE LINE

Contents

Prologue   xi

1. The Voyage of Continent Australia   1
2. Joseph Banks - The Voyage of the Endeavour   14
3. Joseph Banks - In Australia   30
4. Sir Joseph Banks - In London   49
5. Charles Darwin - The Early Years   60
6. Charles Darwin - The Voyage of the Beagle   74
7. Charles Darwin - In Australia   95
8. Charles Darwin - In London   112
9. Alfred Russel Wallace – The Early Years   122
10. Alfred Russel Wallace – The Voyages on the Amazon   132
11. Charles Darwin - At Down House   147
12. Alfred Russel Wallace - In Singapore and Borneo   157
13. Where Australia Collides with Asia   171
14. Wallace's Voyage to Aru Island   179
15. Alfred Russel Wallace - The 'Letter from Ternate'   199
16. Alfred Russel Wallace – The Voyage to Wagio   208

17 Charles Darwin – On the Origin of Species   218
18 Alfred Russel Wallace – The Return to England 232

Epilogue 243
Bibliography 251
Author Note 254
Other Books 257

Portrait of Charles Darwin, Walter William Ouless, 1875

It is interesting to contemplate a tangled bank, clothed with many plants of many kinds, with birds singing in the bushes, with various insects flitting about, and with worms crawling through the damp earth, and to reflect on these elaborately constructed forms, so different from each other, and dependent on each other in is complex a manner, have all been produced by the laws acting around us. These laws, taken in the largest sense, being Growth with reproduction: Inheritance which is almost implied by reproduction: Variability from the indirect and direct action of the external conditions of life, and from the use and disuse; a Ratio of Increase so high as to lead to a Struggle for Life, and as a consequence to Natural Selection, entailing the Divergence of Character and the Extinction of less-improved forms. Thus, from the war of nature, from famine and death, the most exalted object of which we are capable of conceiving, namely, the production of higher animals, directly follows.

I would like to thank my wife, Yusra Zahari Burnet, and my daughters, Miranda and Melissa, who have supported me in all my writing ventures. Thanks go to Toni Pollard and Sia Arnason, who provided invaluable comments on the drafts of this work. Thanks to Jeffrey Mellefont for the image of the coastal traders from Macassar and to Damon Ramsey for his information on the botany of Northern Australia. Thanks also to Russell Darnley OAM, who reviewed the manuscript for Rosenberg Publishing.

My thanks as well to the librarians of the State Library of New South Wales, the Stanton Library in North Sydney, the Willoughby Library in Chatswood and the Indonesian Heritage Library in Jakarta, Indonesia.

Cover design by Miranda Burnet
Cover Image: Le Paradis rouge by Jaques Barraband

Copyright © 2025 by Ian Burnet
All rights reserved. No part of this book may be reproduced in any manner whatsoever without written permission except in the case of brief quotations embodied in critical articles and reviews.

First Edition published in 2017 as 'Where Australia Collides with Asia' by Rosenberg Publishing
Second Edition published in 2025 as 'The Wallace Line' by Alfred Street Press

ISBN 9780645106886 (paperback)
ISBN 9780645106893 (ebook)

Prologue

The volcanoes of Mount Agung on Bali and Mount Rijani on Lombok, their 3000 metre peaks shrouded in cloud, stand like giant sentinels guarding the northern entrance to the Lombok Strait, which separates the Indonesian islands of Bali and Lombok. The strait is only twenty-five kilometres wide, but it plunges to a depth of 2140 metres below sea level. Crossing the Strait can be hazardous, and its turbulent waters are the result of the flow-through of waters between the Pacific and Indian Oceans.

In June 1856, the English naturalist Alfred Russel Wallace crossed the narrow strait. During the few days when he stayed on the north coast of Bali, he saw several birds highly characteristic of Asian ornithology with which he was already familiar and would expect to see on Lombok. After a turbulent crossing and being dumped on the shores of the island, he never saw the same birds again. He found a totally different set of species, most of which were entirely unknown not only in Java, but also in Borneo and Sumatra. Among the commonest birds he found in Lombok were white cockatoos and honeyeaters, which are characteristic of Australia and entirely absent from the western region of the archipelago. Wallace wrote in his book, *The Malay Archipelago*:

> The great contrast between the two divisions of the Archipelago is nowhere so abruptly exhibited as on passing from the island of Bali to that of Lombok, where the two regions are in close proximity ... The strait is here fifteen miles wide, so that we may pass in two hours from one great division of the earth to another, differing as essentially in their animal life as Europe does from America.

Because of the lowering of sea levels during the various Ice Ages, the main islands of Sumatra, Java and Borneo were connected by dry land, and it was the deep Lombok Strait that separated these larger islands sitting on the Asian Continental Shelf from the smaller islands of the eastern archipelago. The Lombok Strait represents the boundary between the fauna of Asia and that of Australia, which was subsequently named the Wallace Line.

On the Asian side of the Wallace Line are the Asian elephant, the rare Javanese rhinoceros, Sumatran tigers and Borneo leopards, all kinds of monkeys, the orangutans of Sumatra and Borneo, and numerous birds specific to Asia. On the Australian side are the marsupials such as the possum-like cuscus and tree kangaroos, as well as birds specific to Australia such as white cockatoos, honeyeaters, brush turkeys and the spectacular birds of paradise. By his observations, Alfred Russel Wallace had made a major contribution to a new science, that of biogeography, or the relationship between zoology and geography.

Eastern Indonesia represents a unique part of the earth's surface, because it is here that four of the earth's great tectonic plates - the Eurasian Plate, the Indo-Australian Plate, the Phillipine Plate and the Pacific Plate are in collision with each other. In the region of Maluku (the Moluccas), these powerful forces fused together volcanic island arcs, continental fragments sheared off from Papua New Guinea, seafloor sediments and coral reefs to create new land, forming the unusually shaped islands of Sulawesi and Halmahera. A subduction zone then formed along the western side of Halmahera, causing volcanoes to erupt out of the sea and spreading a thick layer of volcanic ash across the adjacent islands.

Nature abhors a vacuum, and the rich volcanic soils of these newly emergent islands were quickly populated by coconut trees grown from coconuts washed up on their shores, by plants whose seeds were blown with the winds, by birds and butterflies able to fly from island to island, and by animals and insects drifting on floating trees from island to island. Tropical temperatures and monsoonal rains provided the environment for a diversity of plant, bird and other animal species to thrive and evolve in unique ways. The profusion of islands allowed for a separation in the evolution of different species and became an ideal natural laboratory for scientific study. Alfred Russel Wallace spent five years exploring the tropical forests of Maluku, collecting and studying the birds, butterflies, insects and other animal life of eastern Indonesia.

It was tectonic plate movement that brought these disparate worlds together and in this book, we will follow the voyage of Continent Australia after its separation from Antarctica until its collision with Asia, thus creating the biogeographic region first observed by Alfred Russel Wallace and named Wallacea in his honour.

It was my research into Wallacea and its unique position in the natural world that led me to write about the connections between the epic voyages of natural history taken by Joseph Banks, Charles Darwin and then Alfred Russel Wallace. Here we follow 'The Voyage of the *Endeavour*' , which brought Joseph Banks and Daniel Solander to the shores of Botany Bay, where they became the first naturalists to describe the unique flora and fauna of the Australian continent. We follow 'The Voyage of the *Beagle*', which brought the young naturalist Charles Darwin to South America and the Galapagos Islands before reaching Australia, where he sat on the banks of the Cox's river in New South Wales and began trying to understand the significance of his discoveries. We follow Alfred Russel Wallace when he crosses the Lombok Strait and on his voyage 'Voyage to the Aru Islands' in search of birds of paradise, and his recognition of the significance of the Australian creatures he found there. And we follow the famous 'Letter from Ternate' that Alfred Russel Wallace wrote to Charles Darwin in February 1858, which forced Darwin to finally publish his landmark work *On the Origin of Species*.

1

The Voyage of Continent Australia

The jigsaw puzzle of continental and oceanic plates that make up the earth's surface is in constant motion, driven by the earth's molten core, producing the circulation of rock within the earth's mantle. Moving only centimetres per year, the earth literally quakes as these plates diverge, collide and grind past each other. When they collide, the denser oceanic plates sink under the lighter continental plates, subducting marine sediments deep into the interior of the earth. Here, these water-filled sediments become superheated, and the resultant steam, gas and molten lava can erupt explosively at the earth's surface. Indonesia is the most tectonically active region in the world, and its many volcanoes bring destruction to the people and the environment there, but at the same time, they bring even greater fecundity as the mineral-rich volcanic ash is spread over the region.

Two hundred years ago, two British naturalists working in southern India declared that the rocks they examined in the area of Talcher were of glacial origin. Ridiculed by their colleagues and laughed at by other scientists, they had to wait another twenty years before the discovery of a glacially striated rock pavement decided the issue in their favour. A geological paper written in 1872 suggested this Permian-Carboniferous formation be named Gondwana, after the ancient Kingdom of the Gonds, which is of Dravidian origin and whose descendants still live in the area. Discoveries of similar Permian-Carboniferous formations in Australia, South America and Southern Africa, all containing fossils of the widespread *Glossopteris* fern followed, and in 1885, the name Gondwanaland was introduced to describe a postulated ancient supercontinent.

Alfred Wegener was a German scientist specialising in polar research, astronomy and meteorology. By the time he was thirty-two, he and his brother held the world record for an uninterrupted balloon flight of fifty-two hours. He had earned a doctorate in astronomy, while publishing original research on the subject, had served as a meteorologist on two Danish scientific expeditions to Greenland, and had crossed its mile-high ice sheet on foot. He had written several scientific papers on glaciers based on his own field experiences and had become a Professor of Meteorology at the University of Marburg near Frankfurt, Germany. In 1911, he was examining a new atlas with a friend when he was struck by the apparent match of the coastlines of Africa and South America:

> For hours we examined and admired the magnificent maps. At that point a thought came to me. Does not the east coast of South America fit exactly against the west coast of Africa, as if they had once been joined? The fit is even better if you look at a map of the floor of the Atlantic and compare the edges at the drop-off into the ocean basin, rather than at the present edges of the continents. This is an idea I will have to pursue.

In 1912, Wegener wrote a paper in which he proposed that these continents had once been joined together. According to his model, all the continental landmasses had once been joined into a single supercontinent called Pangea, which subsequently split into the northern landmass of Laurasia and the southern landmass of Gondwana. This split set in motion two separate evolutionary pathways for the earth's flora and fauna. Later movements caused Gondwana to separate into Antarctica, Australia, South America, and Africa, with India rapidly moving north to rejoin the northern landmass.

Wegener's book *The Origin of Continents and Oceans*, published in 1915, was received by a sceptical, even hostile scientific community, but his idea ultimately proved to be one of the greatest geological insights of the century. Wegener based his theory not only on the match of the South American and African continents at the edge of their continental shelves, but also on matching rock types, geological structures and fossils such as the fern-like seed plant *Glossopteris* of the Permian-Carboniferous era, which is found across all the southern continents. The directions of the striations on the glaciated early Permian pavement rocks found in South America, South Africa, Australia and India showed the ice had been moving away from a seemingly impossible source, from the oceans to the south. Wegener then concluded that 270 million years ago, these continents were joined to form a supercontinent centred on Antarctica. He called his revolutionary theory 'Continental Drift' and supposed that the mechanism for this spreading might be the centrifugal force of the earth's rotation.

Wegener's theory of continental drift was never accepted by the majority of geologists because it required the continents to move across the oceans without an obvious mechanism for how this could happen. It was not until the 1960s when seafloor magnetometer measurements showed residual magnetic 'stripes' in the ocean floor extending out parallel to the Mid-Atlantic Ridge and forming a perfect mirror image in both directions, that his theory was fully accepted.

Convection currents within the earth's mantle cause upwelling along the Mid-Atlantic Ridge and the intrusion of magma, forcing the older oceanic material to move away in both directions. As the lava solidifies, iron particles take up the direction of the earth's magnetic field at that time, which can reverse every few hundred thousand years. This movement away from the mid-ocean ridges allows the continents to 'drift' apart by being rafted on top of this very slowly moving oceanic material. Unfortunately, Alfred Wegener never lived to see his theory vindicated, as he died in 1930 at the age of fifty while trekking across the Greenland ice sheet in a courageous attempt to re-supply a weather station.

Dolerite pillars of Cape Raoul, Tasman Peninsula

One hundred and sixty million years ago, the supercontinent of Gondwana lay near the South Pole, where the present continents of Australia, India, Africa and South America were all connected to Antarctica, which at this time was ice-free. As a result of this moderate climate a unique Gondwanaland flora and fauna developed, some of which still survives on these now disconnected continents. About 130 million years ago changes in the circulation of convection currents within the earth's upper mantle started to break Gondwanaland apart. Rifts began to form in its crust like cracks in an eggshell. Molten volcanic rocks were intruded into the rocks along the line of rifting which slowly cooled to form pipes of black dolerite. Millions of years of erosion eventually exposed these dolerites where, for instance, at Cape Raoul on the Tasman Peninsula they point across the Southern Ocean towards similar dolerite cliffs in Antarctica.

Gondwanaland began to break up along these rifts as magma or new oceanic material welled up through the crust and spread out as new ocean floor. Around 60 million years ago the oceanic rift between southern Australia and Antarctica began opening from west to east, and by 50 million years ago the last land link between Tasmania and Antarctica was broken.

The separation of the southern continents from Antarctica allowed ocean currents to circle Antarctica for the first time. As a consequence, Antarctica became cooler and ice-bound, while Australia gradually became hotter and drier as it moved north out of the cloud and rain brought by the winds of the Roaring Forties. Once the continental raft that is Australia-New Guinea began its 50 million-year voyage north towards the equator, its cargo of Gondwanan fauna and flora began to evolve independently of life on the other southern continents. On this raft, primitive creatures still thrive, which are only known as fossils elsewhere on the planet. The oldest known flowering plants in the world survive in their remnant rainforests, and the marsupials have made the continent their own dominion.

The original Gondwanaland floras were much the same as the Jurassic gymnosperm forests, which were dominated by conifers such as the Huon pines, Hoop Pines, and the recently discovered Wollemi Pines, with an understory of seed ferns and an abundance of mosses. However, this was changing with the advance of the flowering plants - a new type of plant which used flowers and their nectar to attract insects, which would then spread the associated pollen. A walk through the cool, damp and dark forests of Southern or Antarctic Beech in the high mountains of the east coast of Australia is to walk back into the realm of Gondwanaland. Light filters down through the forest canopy towards the forest floor, which is covered by rotting logs, mosses and ferns. These huge trees with their broad leaves are some of the earliest flowering plants. Their flowers attracted insects, and later birds and marsupials, which spread their pollen. This new method of reproduction revolutionised the plant world, and as the flowering plants extended their dominion, so did the early marsupials such as the pygmy possums, because these flowers offered energy-rich nectar or buds and fruits to add to their diet of forest floor insects and grubs.

As the continent moved northwards, the primordial Gondwanan forests retreated to be replaced by drier, more open woodlands and grasslands, and the old Gondwanan rainforests only survive now as 'islands' along the cool, wet, high ranges of the east coast of Australia. As patches of rainforest grew short of water, the trees dropped their leaves to reduce transpiration, and more sunlight reached the ground, killing off the understory of ferns and mosses, which had survived there with little light. As the rainforest trees died, eucalypts, acacias and casuarinas moved in to replace them. This caused a gradual change across Australia from rainforest, to closed forest, to open woodlands, to dry eucalyptus scrublands and then to grassy plains. Eucalypts grow in the forests and scrublands, acacias grow as wattle trees in the woodlands, casuarinas on the river banks, banksias in the heathlands, and spinifex grows in the wide dry plains of outback Australia. The Mulga, a common dry country acacia, dispensed with leaves altogether to conserve the very limited supply of moisture. What look like leaves are phyllodes, flattened stems with oil glands and restricted numbers of evaporating pores. The branches of Mulga are usually arranged to channel rain down the trunk to masses of fine root hairs in the soil that can capture the water, which would normally evaporate, before it could soak deep into the soil.

The Australian eucalypts proved very versatile, evolving into a wide variety of trunks, leaves, flowers, fruits and growth habits. This diversity allows the eucalypts to thrive from the coldest alpine regions to the hottest deserts that occur across the Australian continent. There are about 700 species of eucalypts and around 1000 species of wattles found in Australia and New Guinea. The result is that Australia is one of the few countries in the world that is associated with two such large and dominant groups of trees.

The Proteaceae are a Gondwanan species which can be found in Southern Africa, Australia and South America. These were among the earliest flowering plants, and the better-known species amongst them, such as the banksias and grevilleas, have adapted to arid and fire-affected habitats. It is significant that the greatest number of Banksia species occur in southern Western Australia, and closest to where they occur in Southern Africa before the continents split apart. Many of the ancestral species are still found in the tropical rainforests, and the tropical species *Banksia dentata* occurs across Northern Australia, New Guinea and on the island of Aru in Indonesia.

The other dominant Gondwanan flora are the Acacias or wattles, and there are more species of these in Australia than in any other genus. The Acacia also extend to the subtropics of the northern hemisphere, but of the approximate 1300 species, around 1000 of them are native to Australia. The flowers can be balls or spikes varying in colour from almost white, through pale yellow, to a deep gold. It is said that there is a wattle in flower somewhere in Australia every day of the year. Their golden flowers gladden the heart of every Australian, and no other plant lifts their spirit and sense of national pride more than the sight of a group of wattles in golden bloom.

The melaleuca are a genus of plants that includes paperbarks, honey-myrtles and tea trees. Their flowers generally occur in groups, forming a "head" or "spike" resembling a brush used for cleaning bottles, containing up to 80 individual flowers. They are superficially like banksia species, which also have their flowers in a spike, but the structure of individual flowers in the two genera is very different.

The soils of Australia are the poorest and most fragile of any continent, its rainfall the most variable, and its rivers the most ephemeral. It has become a harsh land, and the conservation of moisture has become the hallmark of Australia's plants and animals. The ancestral Gondwanan flora evolved defences such as hard, spiny, or thick leathery leaves to conserve moisture. It is the eucalypts that are best adapted to the arid conditions and nutrient-deficient soils and no other comparable area of land in the world is so completely characterised by a single genus of trees. Almost half of Australia's trees and shrubs belong to just two families - the Myrtaceae which includes the eucalypts, tea-trees and bottlebrushes, and the Acacias or wattles.

Grass grows in abundance on the interior plains of Australia. The explorer Thomas Mitchell, when seeing these vast plains for the first time, considered them beautiful and imagined the millions of sheep that would soon be grazing on these inland grasses. Charles Darwin described the landscape when he reached the Bathurst plains during his visit to Australia in January 1836 as follows:

> Extreme uniformity of the vegetation is the most remarkable feature of the landscape of the greater part of New South Wales. Everywhere we have an open woodland, the ground being partially covered with a very thin pasture, with very little appearance of verdure. The trees nearly all belong to one family, and mostly have their leaves placed in a vertical, instead of, as in Europe, in a nearly horizontal position: the foliage is scanty, and of a peculiar pale green tint, without any gloss. Hence the woods appear light and shadowless.

The plants of Australia were also forged in the fire generated from lightning strikes and later by the Aboriginal people using fire to capture animals for food. Eucalypts encourage fire because of the high volatile oil content in their leaves, but can recover from the hottest fires, and within months, their trunks and main branches start to bristle with new leaf growth. This ability to recover from fire through budding and regrowth from the trunk is unique to the eucalypts. Firestick burning was used by the aborigines to produce a flush of new shoots favoured by grazing marsupials which could be more easily hunted in a contained area. Fire also favours the growth of underground tubers such as yams which formed a staple of the aboriginal diet. Many plants that are destroyed by fire have seeds that will regenerate in their place, for example, banksias hold their seeds in woody fruits that open when the parent plant is burnt, and wattle seeds can lie dormant in the soil for years until germinating in response to heat from fire.

It was around the time of the breakup of Gondwanaland that three lineages of mammals emerged. The most primitive are the egg-laying monotremes such as the platypus which is only found in Australia, and the echidna which is only found in Australia and New Guinea. The second lineage are the marsupials, which raise their young in pouches and are fed by a nipple inside the pouch and are almost exclusively found in Australasia. The third group, the placental mammals, which includes ourselves, had the baby's development take place entirely within the mother's womb and these are mainly found in the northern hemisphere. These are the dominant group of mammals found throughout most of the world, but for some reason, it is the marsupials that have thrived in Australia.

The platypus and the echidna are enigmas of the animal world. If they had been found as fossils, they would have created less astonishment than they do as living creatures. The unusual appearance of the platypus, this egg-laying, duck-billed, beaver-tailed, otter-footed mammal, baffled European naturalists when they first en-

**Platypus, John Lewin
State Library of NSW**

countered it. In fact, when the first platypus skin was sent back to England in 1799 it was considered an elaborate hoax. Monotremes are the most primitive of all mammals, and though possessed of fur and suckling their young, they lay eggs and have many other characteristics in common with reptiles. The oldest fossil found in Australia of a Gondwanan species is the opalised jawbone of a monotreme or platypus-type creature, dated from 110 million years ago and found at Lightning Ridge in New South Wales.

Australia's unique marsupial fauna evolved to cope with a drastically altered climate and increasing environmental stress. The open forest kangaroos of today may have evolved from a lineage that began with pygmy possums living in rainforest trees. These tiny ancestors probably gave rise to the many and diverse marsupials that now populate the continent, the kangaroos, the wallabies, the wombats, the bandicoots, the possums and the koalas, which have all spread to fill almost every available environmental niche and make the continent their own dominion.

In 1894, Robert Broom, who was a Scottish doctor, discovered some fossils in the Wombeyan Caves in New South Wales, which he believed were two new species of marsupials, probably possums that lived 15-20 million years ago. The tiny marsupial he named *Burramys parvus* excited much scientific interest because, although it seemed to be some kind of possum, its jaw contained high-grooved, cheek teeth regarded as characteristic of kangaroos. In 1966, a *Burramys*, now known as a Mountain Pygmy Possum, was found in a ski hut at Mount Hotham in Victoria. Possums live in trees, but the Mountain Pygmy Possum lives on the ground in the boulder fields on the upper slopes of the high mountains, hibernating there over the winter months. Remarkably, a long-thought extinct ancestor of the first Australian ground-dwelling marsupials has been rediscovered as a living animal.

The astonishing fossil finds at Riversleigh, a cattle station northwest of Mount Isa in Queensland, demonstrate the life of the rainforest from 5-25 million years ago. The fossil remains of ancient mammals, birds and reptiles are found in a soft freshwater limestone which has not been compressed and means the animals' remains retain their three-dimensional structure. So far, more than two hundred mammals have been found buried in sediments that accumulated in pools surrounded by a forest rich in Antarctic Beech, and these include more than half the mammals and marsupials found in the Australian rainforest today. This amazing find reveals mammalian evolution across a time span of more than 20 million years, when the surrounding ecosystem was changing from a rich rainforest to a semi-arid grassland community.

The Australian lyrebird was scratching away at leaf litter in the early to mid-Miocene at Riversleigh. This greatest of songbirds can sing for hours while trying to impress female birds, and they are ranked as the best in the world for their 'elaborate, complex and beautiful song'. Australia is called the land of the marsupials, but it is also the land of the songbirds since the Corvidae (crows, ravens, magpies, currawongs, birds of paradise and others) originated in Australia about 55-60 million years ago and it is probable that the world's songbirds originated in the southern hemisphere and some have since spread to the rest of the world.

Only the southern continents have large flightless birds such as the African ostrich, the South American rhea, the Australian emu and the now extinct New Zealand moa, which reflect an origin in Gondwanaland. It is the Australian cassowaries that still live in a form very like that of their Gondwanan ancestors, although they are now restricted to the rainforests of far north Queensland and New Guinea. They hunt for fallen fruits on the forest floor in individual territories, which they aggressively defend against intruders. Their descendants are the large emus that have adapted to life on the grassy plains and which share a common ancestry with the other large flightless birds of Gondwanan origin. Unusual among birds, it is the male emus who incubate the eggs laid by the females, they rarely leave the nest in the eight weeks that it takes to incubate the eggs, and the young stay with their father for another year while learning where to find the best feeding areas.

It had been assumed that many of Australia's other birds originated elsewhere and reached the continent by flight. However, modern DNA analysis has revealed that Australia's song birds are more closely related to one another than to similar species elsewhere in the world, suggesting the existence of early native ancestors living on Gondwanaland. From the discovery of fossil feathers, birds are known to have been present in Australia 120 million years ago, when it was still part of Gondwanaland and even before the first flowering plants appeared. The colourful parrots, so characteristic of Australia, were early occupants, and their beaks evolved to break open banksia cones and gumnuts. The birds of paradise are distinctly Australasian and the males have evolved dazzling plumage and vocal displays designed to impress females, indicating that the owner is the possessor of favoured genes. There are thirty-nine species of this family, most of which live in the rainforests of Papua-New Guinea, however, there are three species living in the rainforests of Northern Australia. These include the Victoria Riflebird, which has velvet black plumage with iridescent green markings and in the breeding season, perches on a clearly visible vantage point with its wings raised while it pivots and sways in an attempt to entice a passing female. Display is central to another group of Australian birds, the bower birds. The male guards and tends to his bower for much of the year, repairing, refurbishing and adding to its decoration. In the breeding season, when a female comes into sight, he will perform his courtship song and dance in an effort to entice a female into his bower. The other uniquely Australasian birds are the mound-builders or megapodes, such as the brush turkey. Their big feet help the males to build large mounds of soil and decaying vegetation on the forest floor, and once the temperature in these mounds reaches a certain level, the female lays her eggs in specially prepared holes inside the mound and leaves the eggs to incubate. The superb lyrebird traces its ancestors to the rainforest and is descended from the same group. The males build mounds but for a different purpose. These are used as stages for its mating dance when the male spreads his lyre-shaped tail feathers and bursts forth in song to attract a suitable mate.

The characteristic smell of burning eucalyptus leaves is thirty-five million years old, and smoking ceremonies believed to have cleansing properties and the ability to ward off bad spirits are still carried out by indigenous Australians at significant cultural events such as births, deaths and 'Welcome to Country'. All Australians gladden to the smell of eucalyptus leaves and they are such an integral part of this continent that no Australian can resist occasionally crushing and smelling a eucalyptus leaf to remind them of their roots in this unique landscape.

The first trained naturalists to reach Australia and describe the unique flora and fauna that had evolved on the continent during its 50 million years of isolation were Joseph Banks and Daniel Solander. They sailed with Lieutenant James Cook on HMB *Endeavour* when he charted the east coast of Australia and landed on the shores of the appropriately named Botany Bay in 1770.

2

Joseph Banks - The Voyage of the Endeavour

Joseph Banks was born in 1743 into a family of wealthy landowners who had no fewer than fourteen country estates in Lincolnshire. He grew up in the Manor at Revesby, surrounded by 340 acres of woods and garden, where, as a young boy, he became very fond of fishing and other country pursuits. He would have had private tutors before being sent to school at Harrow when he was nine years old. Here, his Master describes him as an extremely active boy, much given to play, but who could not be convinced of any reason to study his books. At thirteen, his father sent him to Eton College, where life could be brutal for a sensitive young boy, but fortunately, Banks was big for his age, strong and active. Books were still a problem, but with the help of a tutor, he was able to learn some Latin, and a letter sent to his father at Revesby reads:

> Sir,
> It gives me great pleasure to find you think Master Banks improved. To be able to construe a Latin Author into English with Readiness and Propriety is undoubt-

edly no less necessary than to be able to turn an English one into Latin. They ought indeed to go hand in hand together. And I hope we shall by degrees bring Master Banks to a tolerable perfection in the former; though the Point, which I have hitherto been chiefly labouring, is to improve him in the latter, because of his great Deficiency in that Respect when He came to us.

At fifteen years of age, Joseph Banks underwent a dramatic conversion from a boy interested in only games and sports to someone with an overwhelming interest in nature. He recounts how that summer, after bathing in the river with his friends, he wandered home alone through country lanes whose banks were covered in wildflowers lit by the setting sun. He was so struck by their beauty and perfection that in that moment, he decided to become a student of natural history. Telling himself that 'surely it is more natural to study all these productions of Nature than Greek or Latin'. Further along the lane, he found some old women collecting herbs to be sold to the apothecaries in town. He asked them the names of the different flowers and they agreed for the sum of sixpence to teach him all they knew of the types of wildflowers, their seasons, and where they could be collected. His life now had an aim. It was natural history, and he began collecting as many wildflowers, butterflies, beetles and insects as he could find.

Joseph Banks continued his botanical studies at Oxford University, where he made himself a disciple of the leading botanist of Europe, the great Swedish naturalist Carl Linnaeus. Finding there was no Linnean lecturer in botany at Oxford, he characteristically recruited a Professor from Cambridge at his own expense to lecture to himself and his colleagues. He went down from Oxford in 1764 without completing a degree, which was not uncommon among the gentry, especially as this was also the year he gained his inheritance. This included all his family's landed estates in Lincolnshire, which provided one of the great interests of his life, since farming can be considered as a form of applied botany. With his newfound wealth and position in society, Joseph Banks found he could be both self-indulgent and slightly eccentric, characteristics which he would continue to enjoy throughout his life. After his father had died, his mother bought a house in London near the Chelsea Physic Garden. Here, an older neighbour, John Montagu, became firm friends with the young Banks, and when as Lord Sandwich he gained the position of First Lord of the Admiralty, this friendship was to prove extremely advantageous to Banks.

A spirit of adventure was in Joseph Bank's aristocratic blood and in 1766 he joined a Royal Navy expedition as the Naturalist on the H.M.S. *Niger*, sailing to the remote shores of Labrador and Newfoundland. He made several extended collecting excursions ashore and the plants he brought home formed the beginning of his Herbarium. He employed the botanist Daniel Solander to help classify the specimens collected from this expedition and the botanical artist Sydney Parkinson to draw and paint them.

Daniel Solander was born in Sweden and first studied classics and law, then medicine, before becoming interested in Natural History. He became a protégé of Carl Linnaeus, the Swedish botanist who devised the currently used system of classifying organisms that includes kingdom, phylum, class, order, family, genus and species. In particular, Linnaeus devised a binomial system of classifying plants that grouped plants based on their sexual organs. In his *Systema Natura* published in 1735, he gave species two names, a family name and a personal name in Latin. His system introduced order into the classification of plants and was a triumph of empiricism. The frontispiece of his *Systema Natura* shows Linnaeus in the Garden of Eden applying his binomial nomenclature to all the creatures of the Creation, and he liked to say that 'God created and Linnaeus organised'.

For Linnaeus, it was God who created the laws whereby all plants and animals were perfectly constructed for the environment in which they were found. His 'apostles', including Solander, would travel the world to collect new species from the furthest regions on earth for him to describe, and within his lifetime, Linnaeus completed the monumental task of naming and cataloguing 5600 new plant specimens. Collecting natural history specimens had become an obsession in Victorian England and enthusiasts scoured the countryside for new specimens to add to their collections. Daniel Solander had been recruited from Sweden in 1760 to catalogue private botanical collections in England according to the Linnean system, and within a few years, he became Assistant Keeper at the British Museum.

**Portrait of Carl Linnaeus, Alexander Roslin, 1775
Nationalmuseum, Stockholm**

As British explorers reached Africa, South America and Asia, they felt duty-bound to collect bugs, birds, butterflies and plants to send home. Soon, every far-flung post of the expanding British Empire had its amateur collectors who were looking to make their mark in history by having some previously unidentified species named after them. Country houses, museums, universities and ordinary drawing rooms became filled with specimens from around the globe, carefully arranged in what were known as 'Curiosity Cabinets'.

In 1768, Joseph Banks' name appears as a Fellow of the Royal Society, and it was there that he heard of a planned expedition to the South Seas to observe the Transit of Venus. The astronomer Edmund

Halley had predicted that the transit of the planet Venus, when it crossed between the earth and the sun, would occur in 1769 and he argued convincingly that many careful observations of the transit, taken from widely separated points on the globe would allow scientists to calculate the distance of the earth from the sun and provide a greater understanding of the extent of the solar system.

The command of the expedition was entrusted to Lieutenant James Cook, whose remarkable qualities as a seaman, navigator and cartographer had been proven in his survey of the coast of Newfoundland, where he had carefully observed and recorded an eclipse of the sun, which allowed an accurate determination of the longitude of Newfoundland. It was by Cook's recommendation that *The Earl of Pembroke*, a sturdy coal carrier, was commissioned for the voyage and renamed the HMB *Endeavour*. As a merchant seaman, James Cook had learnt his trade on these tough colliers, stoutly built with a large storage capacity and a flat bottom that drew comparatively little water. He knew they could sail close to shore in only a few fathoms of water, and if necessary, the ship could be easily careened and repaired on a foreign shore.

**Portrait of James Cook, George Nathaniel Dance
National Maritime Museum, London**

Lieutenant Cook was called before the Council of the Royal Society and formally appointed as one of its 'Observers of the Transit of Venus' and Mr Charles Green, an assistant astronomer at the Greenwich Observatory, was appointed to be the 'Second Observer'. The *Endeavour* did not carry the marine chronometer currently being devised by James Harrison and significantly Charles Green was one of the few men besides Cook who could calculate longitude at sea purely from observations of the moon and stars. Green proved a tireless assistant to Cook in checking navigational observations, and the expedition was equipped with two reflecting telescopes, an astronomical quadrant, a brass Hadley's sextant, a barometer, a Journeyman's clock and two thermometers. The Council of the Royal Society recommended that the *Endeavour* sail to Tahiti as the place most suitable for the Southern observations and nominated one of its own Fellows to join the expedition, as explained in this letter:

> Joseph Banks Esq., Fellow of this Society, a gentleman of large fortune, who is well versed in Natural History, being desirous of undertaking the same voyage, the Council very earnestly requests their Lordships, that in regard to Mr Banks' personal merit and for the advancement of useful knowledge, he also, together with his suite, being seven persons (that is eight persons in all) together with their baggage, be received on board the ship under the command of Capt. Cook.

It was Banks' friendship with Lord Sandwich that probably influenced the Admiralty to allow him and his large party to join the voyage, although it was to be at his own expense. He equipped his part of the expedition at a cost of £10,000 and convinced both Daniel Solander and the Finnish botanist Herman Sporing to join the expedition as part of his private party. Joseph Banks aimed to find and classify as many new species as possible and for him this voyage was a golden opportunity. As described in a letter to Linnaeus by John Ellis:

It was written that no people ever went to sea better fitted out for the purpose of Natural History. They have got a fine library of Natural History; they have all sorts of machines for catching and preserving insects; all kinds of nets, trawls, drags and hooks for coral fishing, they have even a curious contraption of a telescope, by which, put into the water, you can see the bottom at a great depth, where it is clear. They have many cases of bottles with ground stoppers of several sizes, to preserve animals in spirits. They have several sorts of salts to surround the seeds; and wax, both beeswax and that of Myrica; besides there are many people whose sole business is to attend them for this very purpose. They have two painters and draughtsmen, and several volunteers who have a tolerable notion of Natural History.

The two painters included Alexander Buchan, a skilled landscape artist who would record images of the lands and people they visited and Sydney Parkinson, a fine young draughtsman who had painted the natural history specimens collected by Banks in Newfoundland. Banks also required two personal assistants and two servants to tend to his needs, as well as his two hunting dogs.

Detail from the painting of the *Endeavour*, Thomas Luny, 1768, National Library of Australia

On August 26th 1768, His Majesty's Barque Endeavour sailed from Plymouth harbour. As the wind filled her sails she left behind a white wake and the cries of seagulls as she began her voyage down the Atlantic and into the Pacific Ocean. In his journal, James Cook reveals the Orders under which they sailed:

I was therefore ordered to proceed direct to Otaheite (Tahiti) and, after the astronomical observations should be completed, to prosecute the design of making discoveries in the South Pacific Ocean by proceeding south as far as latitude of 40 degrees; then if I found no land, to proceed to the west between 40 and 35 degrees till I fell in with New Zealand, which I was to explore and thence to return to England by such route as I should think proper.

After two months sailing down the South Atlantic the *Endeavour* reached Brazil and the Rio de Janeiro to resupply. To Cook's surprise he received a hostile reception as the Portuguese Viceroy did not believe his ridiculous story of how they were bound for the South Pacific to observe the planet Venus passing before the Sun. Although Cook claimed the *Endeavour* was a British naval vessel, she was clearly a merchantman and according to the Portuguese, probably intent on some nefarious purpose. As a result, none of the crew, including Banks and Solander, were allowed ashore except under guard and a Portuguese soldier was assigned to all the boats that brought goods to and from the ship.

The *Endeavour* rounded Cape Horn by sailing through the straits between Staten Island and Tierra del Fuego. It was on Staten Island that Banks and Solander were, for the first time, able to go ashore and collect plants which according to Cook, were still unknown in Europe. This expedition turned into a disaster when on their return the weather suddenly changed, forced to bivouac overnight in freezing temperatures. Bank's personal assistants must have been carrying the 'preserving alcohol' used for specimens and died of hyperthermia when they mistakenly believed that drinking alcohol would keep them warm.

The naturalists shared with Cook the *Endeavour's* great cabin and Banks describes how they worked:

> Seldom was a gale so strong that it interrupted our usual time of study, which lasted from approximately 8 o'clock in the morning, until 2 o'clock in the afternoon, and from 4 or 5 o'clock, when the smell of cooking had vanished. We sat together until it got dark at a big table in the cabin with our draftsman directly opposite us and showed him the manner in which the drawing should be done and also hastily made descriptions of the all the natural history subjects while they were still fresh.

After ten weeks of calm Pacific sailing, the Endeavour reached Tahiti and set anchor within Matavai Bay. Volcanic peaks rose above them and the lush green tropical vegetation of the island descended all the way down to its shores. Around them, the blue waters of its tropical lagoon were alive with native craft full of curious Tahitians. The *Endeavour* was only the third foreign ship to reach the shores of Tahiti, but the charms of its womenfolk were already legendary. The Endeavour was here to observe the Transit of Venus, but it seems that Venus, the Goddess of Love, had already reached these islands and Banks described what he believed to be the islanders' favourite occupation:

> In the Island of Otaheite where Love is the Chief Occupation, the favorite, nay almost the Sole Luxury of the inhabitants; both the bodies and souls of the women are modelled into the utmost perfection for the soft science, idleness, the father of Love reigns here in almost unmolested ease. While we inhabitants of a changeable climate are obliged to Plow, Sow, Harrow, Reap, Thrash, Grind, Knead and Bake our daily bread and each revolving year again to Plow, Sow etc. etc. the Tahitian has but to climb the breadfruit tree and this Leisure is given up to Love.

The crew of the *Endeavour* would also be visited by the Goddess of Love and Cook's first concern on arrival in Tahiti was to draw up a set of rules forbidding all private bartering with the natives by the ship's crew. The price of love could be an iron nail and he drew up a list of rules of conduct, the fifth and last rule being: 'No sort of Iron or anything made of Iron, or any sort of Cloth or other useful or necessary articles are to be given in exchange for anything but provisions'.

Cook knew that bartering for food and supplies must be controlled by one person, and it is a measure of the respect he had already formed for Joseph Banks that he put him in charge of all contact with the Tahitians. In a short time, Banks learned enough of their language to make himself understood, and he was soon in daily contact with the Tahitians to arrange for the resupply of the *Endeavour*. According to Cook:

> Our traffick with these people was carried on with so much order as the best regulated market in Europe. It was managed ashore by Mr Banks, who took uncommon pains to procure from the Natives every kind of refreshment that was to be got.

Banks himself had an eye for dusky maidens as he describes in his own journal. Drawn to the delights offered by the Delta of Venus, he spent most of his nights ashore with the island beauties, practising his language skills. The young Sydney Parkinson was obviously not so smitten and wrote disapprovingly of the activities of his employer and his shipmates:

> Most of our ship's company procured temporary wives amongst the Natives, with whom they occasionally cohabitated; an indulgence which even many reputed virtuous Europeans allow themselves, in uncivilised parts of the world, with impunity. As if a change of place altered the moral turpitude of fornification: and what is a sin in Europe, is only a simple gratification in America; which is to suppose that the obligation of chastity is local, and restricted only to particular parts of the globe.

Notwithstanding so many distractions, the crew prepared a stockade on what they named Point Venus, in which Mr Green could set up his astronomical equipment and readied himself for the all-important observation of the Transit of Venus. Pilfering was a continuing problem for the *Endeavour* especially of anything composed of metal. Despite the stockade being continuously guarded by sentries, the brass quadrant needed for the determination of longitude was stolen and there was no second quadrant in reserve.

This would jeopardise the whole purpose of the expedition. With no observation of the Transit of Venus, the Admiralty and the Royal Society would be acutely embarrassed, there would have to be an official Naval enquiry and there was no doubt that heads would roll. Banks, Green, a midshipman and a Tahitian interpreter set off immediately into the interior of the island in search of the persons who they learned were responsible for the theft. When they reached their village, they found them hostile, following a Tahitian custom Banks quickly drew a circle on the ground and sat down in the middle. Here he began to explain the situation, to quietly negotiate, and after some time the quadrant appeared. To their great relief all the pieces were recovered except for the wooden tripod stand.

The third of June 1769 dawned, this was the day the Transit of Venus was predicted and the weather was perfect. Cook, Green and Solander made their measurements of the transit, as for over an hour a small, dark object moved across the sun's face. However, their telescopes showed a blurred edge around the planet, which meant the observers could not agree on the exact time when Venus entered and left the sun's disc and as Cook writes:

> We very distinctly saw an Atmosphere or dusky shade round the body of the Planet which very much disturbed the times of the Contacts particularly the two internal ones. Dr Solander observed as well as Mr Green and myself, and we differed from one another in observing the times of the Contacts much more than can be expected.

Despite all these other activities, Banks and Solander managed to make an extensive survey of the plant life of the island, collecting, preserving and cataloguing an increasing accumulation of specimens in the three months they were in Tahiti. Regretfully, Alexander Buchan, the landscape artist, died of an epileptic fit while on the island, which was a great loss for the expedition; however, Sydney Parkinson rose to the challenge, and his landscape sketches are full of detail and interest.

During their stay in Tahiti the crew of the *Endeavour* regularly dined on breadfruit, which grew everywhere and was the staple food of the island. It is a good food source, rich in carbohydrates, vitamin C as well as thiamine and potassium. According to Daniel Solander:

The Breadfruit of the South Sea Islands within the Tropics, which was by us during several months, daily eaten as a substitute for Bread, was universally esteemed as palatable and nourishing as Bread itself; no one of the whole ship company complained when served with Breadfruit in lieu of Biscuit; and from the health and strength of whole nations whose principle food it is, I didn't scruple to call it one of the most useful vegetables in the world ... As it undoubtedly must be of the utmost consequence to bring so valuable a Fruit to countries where the climate is favourable to encourage everybody who goes to any part of the world where it is to be met with, bring it over either by young plants properly rooted or by seeds collected in the Proper season, and sown during the passage. I am sure no expense ought to be spared in an undertaking so interesting to the public.

It was almost twenty years later, in 1787, that the now Sir Joseph Banks proposed that an Admiralty vessel be sent to Tahiti to collect breadfruit seedlings and transport them to the West Indies, where they could be grown to feed the plantation slaves. This was the object of the ill-fated expedition of *HMS Bounty* and its commander Captain William Bligh. The ship's great cabin had been converted to accommodate one thousand potted breadfruit plants. However, when they arrived in Tahiti in 1789 it was not the correct season and it took five months before all the breadfruit seedlings were potted and ready for transportation. Unfortunately, during this period, Venus the Goddess of Love, also visited the *Bounty* and it was Captain Bligh's attempts to maintain discipline during this long period that led to his problems with the crew and the resulting 'Mutiny on the Bounty'.

After the observation of the Transit of Venus, Cook followed his instructions from the Admiralty and the *Endeavour* sailed south towards latitude 40 degrees in search of 'The Great South Land'. After sailing into continuous gales, mountainous seas and the increasing cold for 2000 kilometres without sighting any land, the *Endeavour* eagerly turned west. Finally, in October 1769 they sighted land and expectations rose. Could this be a northern promontory of the postulated 'Great South Land' they had been sent to discover? The crew of the *Endeavour* seemed to think it was as Joseph Banks writes:

> At sunset all hands at the mast head, land still distant 7 or 8 leagues, appears larger than ever, in many parts 3, 4 and 5 ranges of hills are seen over the other and a chain of Mountains over all, some of which appear enormously high. Much difference of opinion and many conjectures about islands, rivers etc, but all hands seem to agree that this is certainly the Continent we are in search of.

Cook was more cautious because this could be the east coast of the land discovered by the Dutch explorer Abel Tasman many years before, which he named New Zealand. Tasman found the people of New Zealand to be exceedingly fierce and warlike. His first contact with the Maori took place in 1642 at what he named Murderers' Bay, when four of his crew were killed while passing between their boats. After this encounter, Tasman sailed north without making any further attempts to land. In his journal, Cook describes their first serious encounter with the Maori:

> I landed upon the Island accompanied by Mr Banks and Dr Solander ... Before we could well look about us we were surrounded by two or three hundred people, and, not withstanding that they were all armed they came upon us in such a confused, straggling manner that we hardly suspected that they meant us any harm, but in this we were soon undeceived ... they next attempted to come in upon us, upon which I fired a Musquet loaded with small shot at one of the forwardest of them and Mr Banks and two of the men fired immediately after. This

made them retire back a little, but in less than a minute one of the Chiefs rallied them again. Dr Solander, seeing this, gave him a peppering with small shot, which sent him off and made him retire a second time.

After Cook circumnavigated both the North and South islands, he completely disproved the idea that this was 'The Great South Land' they had been sent to discover. Banks describes how Cook proved 'the total demolition of our aerial fabric called a continent' and now the southern continent seemed more myth than a reality. For Banks, this meant the abandonment of their search and he wrote:

> This for my own part I confess I could not do without much regret – That a Southern Continent really exists, I firmly believe; but if asked why I believe so, I confess my reasons are weak; yet I have a prepossession in favour of the fact which I find it difficult to account for.

Having now completed his instructions from the Admiralty, Lieutenant Cook had to decide how they would return to England. Forever the explorer, he wanted to search for the yet undiscovered east coast of New Holland (Australia), which was unknown anywhere north of Tasmania, or Van Diemen's Land as it was named by Abel Tasman in 1642. To return by way of the East Indies meant he would also have to sail through the uncharted strait that the Spanish explorer Luis Vas de Torres had apparently navigated between New Guinea and New Holland almost two hundred years earlier in 1606. Cook wrote in his journal:

> Being now resolved to quit this Country altogether and to bend my thoughts towards returning home by such a route as might Conduce to the advantage of the Service I am upon, I consulted with the Officers upon the most Eligible way of

putting them in Execution. To return by way of Cape Horn was what I most wished, because by this route we should have been able to prove the existence or non-existence of a Southern Continent which yet remains doubtful; but in order to ascertain this we must have kept in a higher Latitude in the very Depth of Winter but the Condition of the Ship, in every respect was not thought sufficient for such an Undertaking. For the same reason, thoughts of proceeding directly to the Cape of Good Hope were laid aside, especially as no Discovery of any moment could be hoped for in that route. It was therefore decided to return by way of the Indies.. To return by way of the East Indies by the following route: upon leaving this coast to steer westwards until we fall in with the East Coast of New Holland, and then follow the direction of that coast to the northward or what other direction it may take until we arrive at its northern extremity.

3

Joseph Banks - In Australia

In April 1770, after three months sailing west, Cook first sighted the unknown east coast of Australia near the eastern extremity of Victoria at Cape Everard:

> With the first day light this morn the Land was seen, at 10 it was pretty plainly observed; it is made in sloping hills, covered in part with trees or bushed but interspersed with large tracts of sand.

In the afternoon, the crew saw smoke in several places, which led them to believe the country was inhabited. Sailing northward for almost ten days, the *Endeavour* could not find a harbour or safe place to land on the surf-washed coast. An attempt to land near Wollongong had to be aborted because the surf made the landing too risky. Finally, they rounded a Cape and found a sheltered anchorage in what Cook at first called Stingray Bay:

> The land this morn appeared cliffy and barren without wood. An opening appearing like a harbour was seen and we stood directly in for it. A small smoke arising from a very barren place we directed our glasses that way and we soon saw

about 10 people, who on our approach left the fire and retired to a little prominence where they could conveniently see the ship.

Landing of Cook, Banks and Solander at Botany Bay, E.Phillips Fox, 1902, National Gallery of Victoria

When Cook's party first came ashore, their arrival was contested by two aborigines who threw spears at them until they were wounded by gunfire. In the following days, there were other encounters with the aborigines who, at times, appeared threatening, waving their spears at the intruders, but avoiding any direct contact. Even trinkets such as beads, ribbons and cloth, which they tossed to children cowering in a shelter, were ignored. Cloth and beads appeared to be of no practical use to the Australian aborigines as they found them still laying there on the ground the following day, and according to Cook 'all they seemed to want is for us to be gone'. Banks describes the landscape and the colourful birds of this new land which were found to be good eating:

> The soil is a kind of grey sand, there is a variety of flowering shrubs; a tree that yields gum and we saw a great number of birds of a beautiful plumage. Two sorts of parroquets, and a beautiful loriquet, they shot a few of them and they were made into a pie, which the crew said ate very well.

The variety of flowering shrubs was, of course, the banksia, and no other landscape in the world is so dominated by one genus. Coast Banksia (Banksia integrifolia) would have been one of the first trees seen as they came ashore, nearby they found the rugged Saw Banksia (Banksia Serrata) in flower and bearing massive fruiting cones, and the Heath Banksia (Banksia ericifolia) with small narrow leaves and golden-orange flowers.

The crew went ashore to reprovision the *Endeavour*, blunting their axes on the eucalyptus hardwoods while cutting timber for fuel, cutting grass to feed the animals onboard, refilling their casks with fresh water from a small stream, and casting nets to collect the abundant fish and stingray in the shallow waters of the bay. Timber in the form of the 'gum' trees was abundant and Cook described the timber available as:

Banksia Integrifolia

In great plenty, yet there is very little variety; the biggest trees are as large or larger than our Oaks in England, and grow a great deal like them, and yields a reddish gum; the wood itself is heavy, hard and black.

As soon as possible Banks and Solander went ashore to start collecting natural history specimens. They were the first trained naturalists to land on the shores of the Australian continent, full of its ancient and unusual life forms, and they discovered a vast variety of plants which they had never seen before. Banks wrote:

The Captain, Dr Solander, myself and some of the people, making in all ten musquets, resolved to make an excursion into the country. We accordingly did so and walked till we completely tired ourselves, which was in the evening, seeing by the way only one Indian who ran from us as soon as he saw us. The soil wherever we saw it consisted either swamps or light sandy soil on which grew very few species of trees, one of which was large yielding a gum much like 'sanguis draconis', but every place was covered with vast quantities of grass ... The trees over our heads abounded very much with Loriquets and Cocatoos of which we shot several; both these sorts flew in flocks of several scores together.

The botanical findings of Banks and Solander were of great significance since here were genera previously unknown to science, and they struggled with how to classify these new plants. They were the first to see the gnarled bark and whiskered cobs of the *Banksia serrata*, admiring its red-flowered bottle brush, which typifies the unique flora of the continent and they collected three different species of banksia. Banks wrote:

> Our collection of plants was now grown so immensely large that it was necessary that some extraordinary care should be taken of them least they should spoil in the books. I therefore devoted this day to that business and carried all the drying paper, near 200 Quires of which the larger part was full, ashore and spreading them upon a sail in the sun kept them in this manner exposed the whole day, often turning them and sometimes turning the Quires in which were plants inside out. By this means they came on board at night in very good condition.

Parkinson sketched nearly 100 new species of plants, outlining the stem leaf and flower of as many specimens as possible, while making notes of the colours to be painted in later. The gum trees were of great significance but unfortunately they did not make a single drawing of the eucalypts because the rules of botany in 1770 required that floral specimens be drawn with their blossoms and at this time of the year the gum trees were not in flower.

The *Endeavour* remained in the bay for a week. The Union Jack was flown every day and an inscription was cut into one of the trees with the name of the *Endeavour* and the date of its arrival. Initially, Cook had thought to name it Stingray Bay because of their abundance in its shallow waters; however, on their last day, he wrote:

> Sunday 6th. In the evening the yawl returned from fishing having caught two Sting rays weighing near 600 pounds. The great quantity of New Plants etc. Mr Banks and Dr Solander collected in this place occasioned me giving it the name of Botany Bay.

After a week at Botany Bay the *Endeavour* sailed out between what is now known as Cape Banks and Cape Solander and turned north along the coast. For the next month, the botanists were busy drawing and describing their immense collection of new plants while Cook and his crew mapped the coastline. To undertake their mapping, the *Endeavour* would anchor about 2 miles offshore at a good vantage point. From their fixed anchorage, they took bearings of all the visible mountains, headlands and other geographic features as well as sun and star shots to calculate latitude and longitude, before they then sailed on to the next vantage point.

Volcanoes had erupted down the coast of Eastern Australia millions of years ago, emitting ash and basalt that enriched the surrounding soils. A remnant volcanic plug, which Cook named Mount Warning, cautioned him to avoid the rocks jutting out of the north head of the Tweed River. In southern Queensland, remnant volcanic cores stand above the terrain in what Cook named the Glasshouse Mountains, as they reminded him of the chimney cones of the glass foundries he knew in Yorkshire. Further north, they found a bay with good anchorage and on the adjacent sandbanks shot a species of bustard as big as a turkey, which turned out to be good eating, and it was agreed to call the place Bustard Bay. After they passed the Tropic of Capricorn they found some familiar species of tropical plants and Banks writes:

> We landed near the mouth of a large lagoon which ran a good way into the country and sent out a strong tide; here we found a great variety of Plants, several however the same as those we ourselves had before seen in the Islands between the tropics and others known to be natives of the East Indies, a sure mark that we were upon the point of leaving the Southern Temperate Zone and for the future we must expect to meet with plants etc. a part of which at least have been seen by Europeans.

As they continued their voyage northwards, the *Endeavour* and its crew were unknowingly sailing into a trap. The Great Barrier Reef stretches over 2300 kilometres from the Tropic of Capricorn near Townsville to the tip of Cape York at the northernmost point of Australia. The gap between the coast and the reef is widest in the south and gradually narrowed as they sailed north. On the 9th of June, Cook had taken the risk of sailing at night, under a full moon, when at 11 pm the *Endeavour* ran aground and as Cook explains:

> Having the advantage of fine breeze of wind and a clear moon-light night ... we deepened our water from 14 to 21 fathom when all at once we fell into 12, 10 and 8 fathom. At this time I had everybody at their stations to put about and come to an anchor but in this I was not so fortunate for meeting again with deep water I thought there could be no danger in standing on, before 10 o'clock we had 20 and 21 fathom and continued in that depth until a few minutes before 11 and before the man at the lead could heave another cast, the Ship struck and stuck fast.

The *Endeavour* had run aground on a coral reef, which had punched a hole in the keel, and she was rapidly taking on water. The crew, including Banks and his party, worked the pumps all that night, all the next day and again the following night, while trying to keep their vessel afloat. Banks describes their ordeal:

> At night the tide almost floated her but she made waters so fast that three pumps hard worked could but just keep her clear and the 4th absolutely refused to deliver a drop of water. Now in my opinion I entirely gave up the ship and packing up what I thought I might save prepared myself for the worst ... if (as was probable) she should make more water when hauled off she must sink and we well knew that our boats were not capable of carrying us all ashore, so that some, probably the most of us must be drowned.

After lightening the ship of its ballast, guns and other materials, the *Endeavour* floated off on the next high tide and to their great relief, the pumps were still capable of holding the leak. The next day, some of the crew hauled a spare sail under the boat, in a process known as 'fothering', while adding some miscellaneous plugging material (oakum, wool and sheep dung) to try and stop the leak. This was remarkably effective, and within an hour, the water level in the *Endeavour* was almost completely down. Banks was much relieved and impressed with the actions of the captain, officers and crew as he wrote:

> During the whole of this distress I must say for the credit of our people that I believe every man exerted his utmost for the preservation of the ship, contrary to what I have universally heard to be the behaviour of sea men who have commonly, as soon as a ship is in a desperate situation, begin to plunder and refuse all commands. This was no doubt owing to the cool and steady conduct of the officers, who during the whole time never gave an order which did not show them to be perfectly composed and unmoved by the circumstances howsoever dreadful they might appear.

Cook sent the pinnace ahead to try and find a suitable landing place where they could inspect and repair the damage, or if necessary, build a vessel which would carry some of the crew to the East Indies for help. Banks describes the discovery of Endeavour River as almost providential, for the winds had started to blow, and the ship may have sunk had she stayed out a day longer:

> The Captain and myself went ashore to view the Harbour and found it indeed beyond our most sanguine wishes: it was the mouth of a river the entrance of which was to be sure narrow enough and shallow, but once in the ship might be moored

afloat so near the shore ... that all her Cargo might be got out and in again in a very short time.

After careening the *Endeavour*, an inspection of her hull found a hole large enough to have sunk the ship, but providence had worked in their favour as the hole had been plugged with a piece of coral as big as a man's fist. Sydney Parkinson wrote that:

> The same rock, therefore, that endangered us, yielded us the principle means of our redemption; for, had not this fragment not intruded into the leak, in all probability the ship would have sunk.

Repairing the *Endeavour* at Endeavour River
Sydney Parkinson, University of Pittsburgh Library

It would take at least a week to repair the vessel, so sleeping tents, storage tents, a blacksmith's forge, a carpenter's workshop and pens for the animals were set up on shore. Banks and Solander began collecting specimens. Fortunately, the 'gum' trees were now in flower and Parkinson sketched two species of Eucalyptus, the smooth white-barked *Eucalyptus alba* and the narrow-leaved red ironbark, *Eucalyptus crebra*. Despite their numerous landfalls, these were the only sketched example of Eucalypts made during their time in Australia. Parkinson also describes the 'very grateful odour' coming from a fire of burning eucalypts, a smell which was so familiar to the aborigines and to the many subsequent generations of Australian settlers.

A hunting party sent to the other side of the river encountered an unusual animal described as large as a grey-hound, of a mouse colour and very swift. Banks went out on a subsequent hunt and describes another encounter with this strange animal:

> With first dawn we set out in search of Game. We walked many miles over the flats and saw four of the animals, two of which my greyhound fairly chased, but they beat him owing to the length and thickness of the grass which prevented him from running while they at every bound leaped over the tops of it. We observed much to our surprise that instead of going on all fours this animal went only on two legs, making vast bounds.

Next, Banks describes how the second lieutenant who was out shooting another day had the good fortune to kill one of the animals, which had long been the subject of their speculation. Banks wrote 'kanguru' in his diary, his anglicised version of the aboriginal word 'ganurru'. The animal weighed twenty-eight pounds and was eaten for dinner, providing what was described as excellent food, although Banks fails to mention if its bones were preserved for science:

> To compare it to any European animal would be impossible as it has not the least resemblance of any one I have seen. Its fore legs are extremely short and of no use to it in walking, its hind legs are disproportionally long; with these it hops seven or eight feet at each hop.

Parkinson also describes how Banks found an equally unusual creature in the woods, a possum, which had a membranous bag near its stomach where it concealed and carried two young ones sucking at its teat. So we have the first detailed descriptions of the pouch-bearing marsupials that characterise Australian fauna.

During their stay at Endeavour River, the crew made almost daily contact with the local aborigines, but they generally kept out of each other's way. The natives here used outrigger canoes, which were an improvement on the bark canoes the aborigines had used in Botany Bay. They were mainly out catching fish, stingray and turtle, which were also the main food source being gathered by the stranded sailors. The Endeavour crew had the most success in gathering turtles, which were 200 or 300 pounds in weight and seemed to be abundant. The aborigines obviously resented the sailors gathering so many turtles, which was also their primary food source, and Banks described how they were visited by ten aborigines armed with spears:

> They soon let us know their errand, which was by some means or other to get one of our turtles, of which we had 8 or 9 lying upon the decks. They first by signs asked for One and on being refused showed great marks of Resentment; one who had asked me on my refusal stamping with his feet pushed me from him with a countenance full of disdain and applied to some one else; as however they met with no encouragement in this they laid hold of a turtle and hauled him forward to the side of the ship where their canoe lay. It however was soon taken from them and replaced. They nevertheless repeated the experiment 2 or 3 times and after meeting with so many repulses all in an instant leaped into their Canoe and went ashore where I had got before them just ready to set out plant gathering; they seized their arms in an instant, and taking fire from under a pitch kettle which was boiling they began to set fire to the grass to the windward ... the grass which was 4 to 5 feet high and as dry as stubble burnt with vast fury.

Turtles were a prized seasonal food source for the aborigines and to be denied just one, of the many the crew had collected, was an insult that required an act of revenge. Banks already noted that the Aborigines had left the clothes and trinkets they had been given and the sailors found them abandoned in a heap. They seemed to set no value on anything the visitors had except the turtle, which Banks explains they were least able to spare, for this food was necessary for their own survival. The fire could have been a disaster as all their stores and gunpowder were ashore while the *Endeavour* was being repaired, and only that morning the store tent and the sick tent had been loaded on board in readiness for their departure.

Modern DNA studies show that the Australian aborigines are the oldest continuously living population on our planet. They migrated from Africa around 75,000 years ago, they would have reached Australia by island hopping across the Indonesian archipelago during the lowering of sea levels and have been living in Australia for at least 50,000 years. James Cook admired the aborigines he encountered and their life style, as he wrote:

> From what I have said of the natives of New Holland they may appear to some to be the most wretched people upon Earth, but in reality they are far more happier than we Europeans; Being wholly unacquainted not only with the superfluous but the necessary conveniences so sought after in Europe, they are happy in not knowing the use of them ... In short, they seemed to set no value upon anything we gave them, nor would they part with anything of their own for any one article we could offer them; this, in my opinion, argues that they think themselves provided with all the necessaries of life and that they have no superfluities.

Having completed their repairs and after 47 days ashore, the *Endeavour* and its crew were ready to continue their voyage north. If only they could find their way out of the shoals and reefs that surrounded them and Banks wrote in his journal:

**Australian Aborigines,
Sydney Parkinson
National Library of Australia**

Where to go? –to windward was impossible, to leeward was a labyrinth of shoals, so that how soon might we have the ship to repair again, or lose her, quite no one could tell.

For the next week the *Endeavour* threaded its way through the labyrinth of shoals with the pinnace sounding the water depth ahead of them. Eventually they reached Lizard Island, where Cook could climb to the highest point and observe what lay ahead:

> I immediately went upon the highest hill on the island where to my mortification I discovered a Reef of Rocks lying at about 2 or 3 Leagues without the island, extending in a line NW and SE farther than I could see and on which the sea broke very high.

They had indeed sailed into a trap as this was the Great Barrier Reef which extends for 2300 kilometres along the coast of northeast Australia. Fortunately, Cook could see a gap in the line of breakers which might allow a way out through the Barrier Reef, he sent the pinnace ahead to sound the narrow channel, which allowed the *Endeavour* to pass through into the open ocean. For the first time in three months, they were now out of sight of land and safe in deep water, free of all fears of shoals and running aground again. They were now safe, or so they thought. Cook did not want to sail too far out to sea in case he missed sighting the supposed passage between New Holland and New Guinea, and three days later, an easterly swell was driving them back towards the Barrier Reef and the line of breakers they had just escaped from. Banks describes the reef as:

> Something scarcely known in Europe but is a wall of coral rock where the large waves of the vast ocean meeting with so sudden a resistance as to make a terrible mountainous surf, especially in our case where the general trade wind blows directly upon it.

The crew of the *Endeavour* had no way of knowing the difficulties ahead, unless they had read the description by the French explorer Louis Antoine de Bougainville, who with his frigate *La Boudeuse* had approached the reef directly from the east only a few years earlier. The tremendous roar of the surf breaking across the reef gave Bougainville enough warning to haul away, describing the roar of the surf and their lucky escape he wrote 'This was the voice of God, and we obeyed it'. At daybreak, the roar of the surf was plainly heard by James Cook and the vast foaming breakers could be seen only a few kilometres away. There was no wind to allow them to haul away and the ocean current was relentlessly carrying the *Endeavour* towards the outer edge of the Great Barrier Reef. Joseph Banks describes their situation as desperate:

> At three o'clock this morn it dropped calm on a sudden which did not at all better our situation; we judged ourselves not more than 4 or 5 leagues from the reef, maybe much less,

and the swell of the sea which drove right in upon it carried the ship towards it fast ... as day broke the vast foaming billows were plainly enough to be seen scarce a mile from us and towards which we found the ship carried by the waves surprisingly fast ... Now was our case truly desperate, no man I believe but who gave himself entirely over, a speedy death was all we had to hope for and that from the vastness of the breakers which must quickly dash the ship all to pieces - was scarce to be doubted.

They were now almost upon the reef. Cook describes how the ship rose up to a prodigious height with one breaker and that between them and destruction was only a dismal valley the breadth of one wave. Then, what Banks describes as a little breeze came up from the west, which halted their progress and using their sails, they were able to move in a slanting direction away from the Barrier Reef until they saw a narrow break in the reef ahead. The pinnace was sent to scout the opening and came back with the news that although it was very narrow, the passage was quite free from shoals. Banks describes how they were again saved from disaster:

> The ships' head was immediately put towards it and with the tide she towed fast so that by three we entered and were hurried in by a stream almost like a mill race, which kept us from even a fear of the sides, though it was not above ¼ of a mile in breadth. By 4pm we came to an anchor happy once more to encounter those shoals which but two days before we thought ourselves supremely happy to have escaped from. How little do men know what is for their real advantage: two days ago our utmost wishes were crowned by getting without the reef and today we were made happy again by getting within it.

For once, James Cook allowed his emotions to be recorded in his journal, because he wrote that it pleased GOD at this juncture to send us a light air of wind and he named the gap in the reef that saved them Providential Channel.

However, the *Endeavour* still had to make its way through the reefs and shoals of the Torres Strait that separates Australia from Papua-New Guinea. Cook had on board a map prepared by Alexander Dalrymple, the hydrographer to the Royal Navy, which indicated the voyage thought to be made between Australia and Papua-New Guinea by the Spanish explorer Luis Vas de Torres in 1606. The *Endeavour* passed the Cape, which Cook named after the Duke of York, found a passage through the Torres Strait and then what was later named Endeavour Strait into the 'Indian Sea'.

Before leaving Australia, Cook sent a party ashore to what he named Possession Island, hoisting the English colours, he claimed the east coast of Australia for King George III, naming it New South Wales. 'I now once More, hoisted English Colours & in the Name of His Majesty King George the Third took possession of the whole Eastern coast by the Name of New South Wales together with all the Bays Harbours Rivers & Islands situate upon the same Coast'.

Cook had now achieved his objective of exploring the previously uncharted east coast of New Holland and navigating a passage between Australia and Papua-New Guinea:

> We got to the westward of Carpentaria or the northern extremity of New- Holland and now had an open Sea to the westward, which gave me no small satisfaction not only because the dangers and fatigues of the Voyage was drawing near to an end, but by being able to prove that New-Holland and New-Guinea are separate lands or islands, which until this day hath been a doubtful point with Geographers.

After so many years at sea and after almost twice being shipwrecked on the Great Barrier Reef, they were now, to the relief of all on board in charted waters and sailing for home. Banks felt the same relief as all of the crew and as they left Possession Island, he wrote:

> As soon as the boat was hoisted in, we made sail and steered away from this land to the no small satisfaction of I believe three fourths of our company, the sick became well and the melancholy looked gay. The greatest part of them were now pretty far gone with the longing for home which the Physicians have gone so far as to esteem a disease under the name of Nostalgia; indeed I can find hardly anybody in the ship clear of its effects but the Captain, Dr Solander and myself, indeed we three have pretty constant employment for our minds which I believe to be the best if not the only remedy for it.

James Cook had explored and mapped the east coast of Australia. An entire continent populated by the Australian aborigines, covered with sparsely clad eucalypts and acacias, filled with the riotous shrieks of colourful birds and strange pouched marsupials had now been defined. Joseph Banks wrote a summary of their discoveries into his journal:

> For the whole length of coast which we sailed along there was a sameness to be observed in the face of the country very uncommon: Barren it may justly be called and in a very high degree, that at least what we saw. The soil in general is sandy and very light: on it grows grass tall enough but thin set, and trees of tolerable size, never however near together, in general 40, 50, or 60 feet asunder.
> ... Water is here a scarce article or at least was so while we were there, which I believe to have been in the very height of

the Dry season; some places we were in we saw not a drop, and at the two places we filled for the ships use it was done from pools not brooks.

... Of Plants in general the country afforded a far larger variety than its barren appearance seemed to promise. Many of these have no doubt properties which might be useful, but for physical and economic purposes which we were not able to investigate, could we have understood the Indians or made them by any means our friends we might perchance have learned some of these; for though their manner of life, but one degree removed from brutes, does not seem to promise much yet they had a knowledge of plants as we plainly could perceive by having names for them.

... Quadrupeds we saw few and were able to catch few of them we did see. The largest was called by the natives Kangooroo that we did see. It is different from any European and indeed any animal I have heard or read of except the Gerbua of Egypt, which is not larger than a rat when this is as large as a middling lamb.

... Upon the whole, New Holland is in every respect the most barren country I have seen, is not so bad but that between the productions of the sea and land a company of People who should have the misfortune of being shipwrecked upon it might support themselves, even by the resources we have seen. Undoubtedly a longer stay and visiting different parts would discover more.

This immense tract of Land, the largest known which does not bear the name of a continent, as it is considerably larger than all Europe, is thinly inhabited even to admiration, at least that part of it that we saw: we never but once saw so many as thirty Indians together and that was a family.

According to Banks they had discovered a completely new existence which he believed had been formed after the established order of the northern hemisphere.

4

Sir Joseph Banks - In London

The voyage of the *Endeavour* was considered a huge success, notwithstanding its almost fatal encounter with Endeavour Reef. The *Endeavour* had spent more than two years at sea without any of the crew contracting scurvy, thanks to the diet provided by Cook and all the breadfruit they ate in Tahiti. However, the three months the crew stayed in Batavia while the *Endeavour* was being repaired for the voyage back to England were a disaster. Seven crew members died in this cholera-ridden city, and another seventeen died after they sailed for Cape Town. Cook wrote:

> Batavia, I firmly believe is the death of more Europeans than any other place upon the globe ... We came here with as healthy a ship's company as need to go to sea and after a stay of not quite three months left in the condition of a Hospital Ship.

Of Banks' original party of eight, only three survived the voyage. His Negro servants, Richmond and Dorlton, both perished in the snows of Tierra del Fuego. The artist Alexander Buchan died of epilepsy in Tahiti, and Sydney Parkinson and the naturalist's assistant Herman Sporing died from cholera contracted in Batavia.

After their return to England, James Cook was presented to King George III and promoted to master and commander. Banks and Solander were received by the King at Windsor Castle and travelled up to Oxford to receive honorary degrees. The voyage had collected examples of the flora and fauna from an entirely new continent, and before his untimely death, Sydney Parkinson had made 674 outline drawings and 269 finished paintings of their botanical specimens. Banks and Solander reaped both social glory and scientific acclaim, and invitations were forthcoming from the greatest houses in the land. John Ellis wrote to Carl Linnaeus saying that Banks and Solander had returned laden with the greatest treasures of Natural History that were ever brought to England. It was Linnaeus himself who addressed a letter to 'the immortal Banks' and, on behalf of all botanists, thanked God for having brought Banks and Solander safely through all their perils:

> Thanks and glory to God, who has protected him through the dangers of such a voyage! If I were not bound fast here by 64 years of age, and a worn-out body, I would this very day set out for London, to see this great hero of botany.

From the moment they had safely returned to England, Linnaeus and many other scholars wanted to know – when was Banks going to publish his account of the voyage? Was Solander at work on the catalogue? When would the descriptions and the classifications of these new plants be published? The whole botanical world was waiting in anticipation, for in the botanical world defined by Carl Linnaeus, a plant did not officially exist until it was described and classified under the Linnean system and the results published.

But Joseph Banks was now a celebrity and he made himself very much available to the popular press. Banks enjoyed being famous and this started to take up a large part of his time. Fame was certainly more interesting than the tedious job of describing, drawing, and classifying the thousands of plant specimens required to publish a scholarly volume. The increasing view of him as the leading figure of the voyage allowed a newspaper to publish an article referring to 'Lieutenant Cook of the Royal Navy, who sailed around the Globe with Messrs Banks and Solander'. To add to his status, a portrait of Joseph Banks made at the time shows him wearing the cloak of a Maori chief made from native New Zealand flax, over a blue naval uniform with its gold buttons, surrounded by plants, weapons and other souvenirs from the voyage.

Since Banks had no time or possibly no interest in writing his journal of the voyage of the *Endeavour*, Lord Sandwich commissioned a Mr Hawkesworth to write the official narrative of the voyage. Here was a great adventure story. All that was required to achieve huge interest was accuracy, objectivity and the ability to assemble a vivid narrative. It is said that after two years labour Hawkesworth managed to achieve none of these and copies of his *Voyage of the Endeavour* remained unsold.

Portrait of Joseph Banks, Benjamin West
Usher Gallery, Lincoln

While the scientific and botanical world waited to read Banks' account of the voyage and the descriptions of his marvellous specimens, Banks was not only enjoying being famous but suddenly saw another opportunity to add to his glory. In November of that year Cook was appointed to command a second expedition to the

South Seas in a further attempt to discover 'The Great South Land'. He would command the collier renamed *Resolution* with another collier, *Adventurer*, as consort, to leave in March 1772. Through his connections Banks secured an invitation to participate in this next voyage and he wrote:

> Soon after returning from my voyage around the world I was solicited by Lord Sandwich, the First Lord of the Admiralty, to undertake another voyage of the same nature. His solicitation was couched in the following words, "If you will go, we will send other ships." So strong a solicitation, agreeing exactly with my own desires was not to be neglected. I accordingly answered that I was ready and willing.

Banks had returned to England with about 30,000 plant species, of which 1400 were new to science, as well as about 1000 species of animals, birds, fish, insects, etc., which all required careful study. This news of another expedition, and the delay in describing these new specimens, sent the elderly Linnaeus into a fit of despair. With so much work to be done on the first collection, why were Banks and Solander readying to depart on another dangerous voyage around the world? He replied to his friend John Ellis who had sent him this news from England:

> This report has affected me so much as to almost entirely deprive me of my sleep. How vain are the hopes of man! Whilst the whole botanical world, like myself, have been looking for the most transcendent benefits to our science, from the unrivalled exertions of your countrymen, all their matchless and truly astonishing collection, such as has never been seen before, nor may ever be seen again, is to be put aside untouched, to be thrust into some corner, to become the prey of insects and destruction ... I therefore once more beg, nay I earnestly beseech

you, to urge the publication of these new discoveries. I confess it to be my most ardent wish to see this done before I die.

Linnaeus wrote to Solander begging him to stay and catalogue the specimens from Australia, but for whatever reason, Solander never answered his letters. Solander has been described as a 'rather charming fellow, radiant with good feeling, yet constitutionally almost incapable of answering a letter, or of even opening a good many'. Ultimately, Linnaeus had to resign himself to the fact that 'an ungrateful Solander' would not respond to his letters nor send him 'one single herb or insect of all those he collected in Insulis australibus novis'. Eventually, some duplicate specimens were sent to Sweden. The *Banksia serrata* is regarded as the 'type species' of the Banksia, and it was Linnaeus's son Carl who first published the name 'Banksia' and thus commemorated Joseph Banks with his descriptions of three species found at Botany Bay and another at Endeavour River. It was after the death of Carl Linnaeus in 1788 that Banks instigated the acquisition of his entire precisely catalogued collection, and the Linnean Society of London was formed.

Banks' party for this second expedition was to include sixteen people, three draughtsmen, two secretaries, two musicians and nine servants –'all practised and taught by myself to collect such objects of Natural History as might occur' plus himself, his mistress, and Dr Solander. The mistress was a mysterious 'Mr Burnett' who tried to board the ship in Madeira disguised as a man, only to find, to her embarrassed surprise, that Banks was not on board. An incident that a rather bemused Captain James Cook probably had some delight in reporting to the British Admiralty. All these additional people needed to be accommodated in the manner to which they were accustomed, and this required adding a spar deck over the deep waist of the *Resolution* from quarter deck to forecastle for all the 'gentlemen passengers'. The result was that the vessel proved to be completely unseaworthy on its sea trials. No doubt James Cook could see where all this was headed and he wrote to the Admiralty:

> The *Resolution* ship under my command was found upon trial to be so crank that she would not bear her proper sail to be set on her, I give it as my opinion that it was owing to the additional works that have been built on her in order to make large accommodation for the several gentlemen passengers intended to embark upon her and I propose that she might be cut down to her original.

Banks was now suddenly deprived of his special accommodation and, in a fit, refused to go, demanding that his party's enormous amount of baggage and scientific equipment be removed from the ship. He wrote a letter complaining to Lord Sandwich, who forwarded his letter to the Navy Board for comment, and they tersely replied:

> Mr Banks seems throughout to consider the ships as fitted out wholly for his use; the whole undertaking to depend on him and his people; and himself as the Director and Conductor of the whole; for which he is not qualified and if granted to him would have been the greatest disgrace that could be put on his Majesty's Naval Officers.

Banks was incensed. He had already committed his funds and his gentlemen passengers to an expedition, so with Dr Solander they sailed to Iceland in the *Sir Lawrence,* a vessel he chartered, to observe the volcanoes and collect the sparse plants that grow in that barren environment. Banks wrote that the country has 'been visited but seldom and never at all by any good naturalist to my knowledge', but his journal of the voyage is mainly concerned with his continuing grievances against the Navy Board.

On his return to England, Banks could now devote his energy to the enormous amount of work needed to store and describe his vast collection of plants, mammals, reptiles, birds, insects and marine creatures. Solander had written a great many descriptions whilst on board, but there were still many additional ones to be done. The drawings made by the unfortunate Sydney Parkinson had to be completed because he usually made a quick drawing of each specimen, with an indication of the colours to be painted later. The results of the historic Endeavour voyage with all its previously unknown specimens required an equally great publication for the benefit of the learned world. What Banks had in mind was a truly heroic publication, a massive *Florilegium* with no fewer than 743 plates based on Parkinson's finished drawings, with a large amount of descriptive text, in a format that was 18 inches by 12 inches and would require multiple volumes.

By December 1772, his collections were unpacked, prepared and arranged at his house in New Burlington Street, including the 1400 new species that had never been seen in Europe before. This was not a contribution to science as we would expect today, but a gentleman's private collection, for Banks had funded the botanical part of the expedition himself, and his collection was now the greatest 'cabinet of curiosities' in the world. To be ushered into his Herbarium was a special privilege and we have Rev. W. Sheffield's description of his visit published in Gilbert White's *Natural History of Selbourne*:

> The number of plants is about 3000, 110 of which are new genera, and 1400 new species which were never seen or heard of before in Europe. What raptures must they have felt to land upon countries where everything was new to them! Whole forests of not yet described trees clothed with the most beautiful flowers and foliage, and these too inhabited by several curious species of birds equally strangers to them ... Add to these the choicest collection of drawings in Natural History that perhaps ever enriched any cabinet, public or private :- 987 plants

drawn and coloured by Parkinson; and 1300 or 1400 more drawn with each of them a flower, a leaf, and a portion of the stalk, coloured by the same hand; besides a number of other drawings of animals, birds, fish, etc. and what is more extraordinary still, all of the new genera and species contained in this vast collection are accurately described, the descriptions fairly transcribed and fit to be put to press.

Any botanist visiting London would want to go to Banks house in New Burlington Street – later to be exchanged for a grander house at 32 Soho Square - to see his expansive private collection. Interestingly, the specimens of the gum trees were not named by Banks or Solander but by the French botanist Charles Louis L'Héritier de Brutelle who liked trees because – 'they are the part that is most neglected by all botanists'. It was David Nelson who collected a eucalypt on Bruny Island, southern Tasmania, in 1777 on Cook's third expedition. This specimen was taken to the British Museum, where Charles Louis L'Héritier de Brutelle was able to examine the smooth egg-shaped casing around the developing eucalyptus flower buds. Rather than Latin, he thought of the Greek word eu, meaning well, and klyptus, meaning covered, and since the leaves were quite asymmetrical, this suggested *obliqua*, so he started a new genus by calling it *Eucalyptus obliqua*. This name was first published in 1788 and long after the return of Banks and the *Endeavour*.

Joseph Banks continued to have many other interests. In 1778, he was elected President of the Royal Society, a position he held for the next 41 years. He had formed a close friendship with King George III, who named him a Baronet. He was described as the King's 'Minister of Science', since, besides being President of the Royal Society, he was an adviser to the Kew Gardens, on the Board of Agriculture, oversaw the Royal Greenwich Observatory and was a Trustee of the British Museum. In 1779, Banks gave evidence before a committee of the House of Commons where he stated that the place most eligible for the reception of convicts sentenced to transportation was Botany Bay on the coast of New Holland. In this Banks was aided by James Matra, a junior officer on the *Endeavour* who produced 'A Proposal for Establishing a Settlement in New South Wales'. As well as all these activities, Banks had the rounds of London's social life and his farming and property interests. His house at Soho Square became a court, a centre for scientists and the exchange of ideas, but it is said that he 'readily swallowed gross flattery'.

There was a great deal of work to be done on the *Florilegium*, yet ten years after the return of the *Endeavour*, it was still not complete. Daniel Solander had provided twenty manuscript volumes of description, which were prepared for publication and in 1782, Banks wrote that he soon hoped to publish his massive work:

> The botanical work with which I am presently involved is nearing completion. Because everything was produced by our common effort, Solander's name will appear on the title page next to mine ... since all descriptions were made when the plants were fresh, nothing remains to be done, except to fully work out the drawings still to be finished ... All that is left is so little that it can be completed in two months; if only the engravers can put the finishing touches to it.

That same year Banks received a dreadful blow when Daniel Solander, his friend and collaborator, upon whom he relied to complete the *Florilegium*, died of a stroke. Although Banks was his employer and patron, a letter written after Solander's death describes their close personal relationship:

> Through his death I have suffered a loss which will be impossible for me to fill even if I should find another person as learned and as noble ... it is not possible for my heart to replace

the impression which twenty years ago it took as easily as wax and which now will not be effaced until the heart itself dies.

Trial proofs of the *Florilegium* had been bound with the original drawings and sketches, an immense amount of money and effort had been expended on the plates alone. Yet, it is a mystery why it was never published. The voyage could be considered as Banks' greatest achievement yet why could he not bring himself to publish? Publication would have confirmed Banks and Solander's scientific reputations. Solander's important contribution to science would have been remembered for Banks had acknowledged that 'Solander's name will appear on the title page beside mine, since everything was written through our combined labour'.

Plate of Banksia Serrata prepared for the Florilegium 1783 National Museum of Australia

Sir Joseph Banks died almost forty years later in 1820 without his great work having ever been published. He bequeathed to his librarian, Robert Brown, a lifetime interest in his house and his library. His botanical collections went to the Linnean Society, which eventually passed them on to the British Museum, and the collection then moved to the new Natural History Museum after it opened in 1881.

The plates remained in storage and gathering dust for the next two hundred years until Alecto Historical Editions and the British Museum decided to print the complete set of images. In the 1980's a superb limited edition of 100 copies of the *Banks' Florilegium* was published in 34 full colour volumes from the renovated original copper printing plates. The volumes are a magnificent tribute to Joseph Banks, Daniel Solander and Sydney Parkinson, who had collected, described and drawn this material two centuries before, but never saw the completed results of their labour.

Ten years after the death of Sir Joseph Banks another expedition was preparing to leave England for South America, Australia and to circumnavigate the world. The object of the expedition was to complete the survey of the coastlines of Patagonia and Tierra del Fuego commenced under Captain Pringle Stokes from 1826 to 1830, and to survey the coastlines of Chile and Peru. The expedition would also establish for the first time a global network of latitude and longitude measurements at specific ports around the world using the new seaborne chronometers developed by John Harrison. It so happened that a young, inexperienced naturalist named Charles Darwin had been recruited to join the voyage as a dining companion for the ship's captain, Robert FitzRoy.

5

Charles Darwin - The Early Years

Charles Darwin, born in 1809, was the fifth child of Robert Darwin, a prosperous local doctor living in Shrewsbury, the county town of Shropshire. Charles was also the grandson of Erasmus Darwin, one of the most famous men in England, who was not only a doctor but also a noted poet, inventor and natural scientist. Erasmus Darwin formed the Lichfield Botanical Society, which, despite its name, comprised only three men, to translate the works of the Swedish botanist Carl Linnaeus from Latin into English. This took seven years, and the result was two publications: *A System of Vegetables* between 1783 and 1785, and *The Families of Plants* in 1787. Erasmus Darwin was also one of the first people to suggest that existing species might have evolved from earlier life, an idea which he expressed in verse:

> Organic life beneath the shoreless waves
> Was born and nurs'd in oceans pearly caves;
> First, forms minute, unseen by spheric glass
> Move on the mud, or pierce the watery mass;
> These, as successive generations bloom,
> New powers acquire and larger limbs assume;

> Whence countless groups of vegetation spring
> And breathing realms of fin and feet and wing.
>
> Erasmus Darwin. 'The Temple of Nature', 1803

Charles Darwin remembered his childhood as very happy, even though his mother, Susannah Wedgwood, died when he was only eight years old. His three older sisters took over his early education and doted on their little 'Bobby'. On his tenth birthday, he was sent off to a nearby boarding school, but would run home when his lessons were over to spend a delightful hour or two with his sisters. The young Darwin showed a special interest in the world of the fields around him. He joined the Victorian mania for collecting natural history specimens and he found beetles, butterflies, rocks, fossils, ferns, flowers, all to be taken home, described, catalogued and displayed in cabinets. Such was his interest in the natural world that he wrote, 'I could not understand why every gentleman was not an ornithologist'. It was telling that he used the word gentleman because as he entered his teens, he would have understood that because of the accumulated wealth of the Darwin and Wedgwood families, he would never need to work for a living.

Dr Robert Darwin sent his son to Edinburgh at the age of sixteen to study medicine in the hope that he would become a doctor like himself, but it soon became evident that Charles was never going to follow in the footsteps of his father and grandfather. Long before the age of anaesthetics, Charles Darwin found the gruesome realities of nineteenth-century medicine particularly upsetting. As part of his course, he was required to attend the operating theatre in the hospital at Edinburgh. He was so horrified that he had to leave the building and quickly decided he could never become a doctor.

Fortunately, Edinburgh University was the leading centre in Britain for both medicine and science. Unable to admit his aversion to medicine to his father, Darwin took chemistry, natural history and geology classes. He became interested in observing soft-bodied marine organisms collected in Leith harbour and made his first scientific discovery when he found that under the microscope the 'ova' of a gelatinous sea-mat were not eggs at all but free-swimming larvae. At the end of his University year, Darwin had to come home and explain to his father that he had given up his medical studies. Apart from his interest in natural history, he enjoyed shooting and hunting more than anything else and his father was furious, writing:

> You care for nothing but shooting, dogs, and rat-catching, and you will be a disgrace to yourself and all your family.

Even though he would never have to work for a living, his father insisted his son prepare for a career. The Army, Navy or the Law were out of the question, but scattered across England were numerous country parsons who spent their idle hours collecting and studying the natural world around them. His father decided Charles should leave Edinburgh for an education at Christ's College, Cambridge. There he would read for an 'ordinary degree', a syllabus of mathematics, theology, and classical works which was the usual starting point for taking Holy Orders in the Anglican Church. Many clergy devoted themselves to natural history because it filled in their time in a quiet country parish, and they believed that a study of the natural world would bring them to a closer understanding of God, the Creator of all things. An appointment to the right parish might be perfect for Charles, allowing him to shoot with the gentry, ride with the local hunt, then botanise and geologise to his heart's content between the Sunday services. Darwin's inspiration was perhaps the Reverend Gilbert White, the author of the popular book *The Natural History of Selbourne,* who had recorded the plants, birds and animals of a small country parish in Hampshire. This interest in both religion and natural history was best expressed by Sir Francis Bacon when he wrote:

> There are two books laid before us to study, to prevent our falling into error; first, the volume of the Scriptures, which reveal the will of God; then the volume of the Creatures, which express his power.

Although there was much theological argument about the interpretation of the Bible, the description of the origin of life in the Book of Genesis was sacrosanct. The world had been created by God in six days, man had been made in His image, all the creatures of the earth had sprung into existence at the same instant, and had survived the flood only because Noah had taken two of each species, a male and a female, aboard the Ark.

While at Cambridge, Darwin moved into the same rooms as previously occupied by the renowned theologian William Paley, who had in 1802 published a book called *Natural Theology*. Darwin appreciated the clarity and logic of his language and was guided by the ideas of Paley, who had become famous because of his 'Argument for Design':

> Suppose someone wandering across a heath should find a watch lying in his path. He would know at once that it was a manufactured object, from the intricacy of its design. Such an object could not have arisen by chance. Design implies a designer. As it was with the watch, so it was with the natural world. Something so elaborate, so perfectly functioning could not have been produced by the operation of aimless forces; there must have been a Creator.

Darwin's lecture schedule at Cambridge was relatively undemanding, and with his friends, he could follow his passions of game hunting and beetle collecting. Darwin gives an example of his collecting zeal as when tearing off some old bark he saw two rare beetles, then seeing a third and equally rare beetle, and having no more hands he popped one inside his mouth, whereupon it ejected some intensely acrid fluid, forcing him to bend over in disgust, spit it out, and consequently lost all three beetles. His collecting led to him to make a minor contribution to an authoritative textbook and he excitedly wrote:

> No pursuit at Cambridge was followed with nearly so much eagerness or gave me so much pleasure as collecting beetles. It was the mere passion for collecting, for I did not dissect them and rarely compared their external characters with published descriptions, but got them named anyhow ... No poet ever felt more delight at seeing his first poem published than I did at seeing in Stephens' *Illustrations of British Insects* the magic words, 'captured by C.Darwin, Esq.'

While at Cambridge, Darwin formed a friendship with Reverend John Henslow, the Professor of Botany, who encouraged him to attend botany lectures, weekend naturalist outings and consider a clerical career. Darwin acknowledges his assistance in the preface to his book *The Voyage of the Beagle*:

> I must be here allowed to return my most sincere thanks to the Reverend Professor Henslow, who, when I was an undergraduate at Cambridge, was one of the chief means of giving me a taste for natural history, and who, during my absence, took charge of the collections I sent home, and by his correspondence directed my endeavours. It was he who, since my return, has constantly rendered me every assistance which the kindest friend could offer.

Darwin considered himself hopeless at mathematics and hated the classics, but he managed to gain a creditable pass in his final year. Of his academic career, he wrote, 'During the three years which I spent at Cambridge, my time was wasted ... as completely as at Edinburgh and at school'. His real interest was in natural history and he was entranced by the book *Personal Narrative of Travels to the Equinoctial Regions of the New Continent* by the German explorer Alexander von Humboldt, which describes his five years and 15,000 kilometres of travel in South America between 1796 and 1801, with his travelling companion Aimé Bonpland. During their travels, a mule carried a trunk containing their scientific instruments - a compass, a sextant to measure latitude and longitude, an instrument to measure magnetic variation, a thermometer, a barometer and an instrument to measure humidity.

Humboldt conceived a bold new vision of nature that still influences the way we understand the natural world today, as he saw the earth as one great living organism where everything was connected. He conceived the concept of the web of life and saw how plants, animals and humans are connected through the food chain. In Venezuela he describes the devastating effects of deforestation caused by colonial plantations. Climbing Mount Chimborazo in Peru he came up with the idea of climatic zones and noted the corresponding changes in vegetation as he climbed higher up the mountain:

> We were constantly climbing through clouds. In many places, the ridge was not wider than eight or ten inches. To our left was a precipice of snow whose frozen crust glistened like glass. On our right lay a fearful abyss, from 800 to 1000 feet deep, huge masses of rocks projecting from it ... A few rock lichens were seen above the snow lines, at a height of 16,920 feet. The last green moss we noticed about 2,600 feet lower down. A butterfly was captured by M.Bonpland at a height of 15,000 feet and a fly was seen 1600 feet higher.

Humboldt sampled the waters of the different rivers because the Indians could tell the difference by taste, and he tasted the bark of different trees because again, the Indians could tell the difference by taste. Humboldt was interested in everything in the natural world - plants, animals, birds, rocks and water.

Back in Europe, Humboldt published his *Essay on the Geography of Plants*, the first volume of what was to become his thirty-four-volume *Personal Narrative of Travels*. However, his most popular book was *Views of Nature* in which he combined his observations of natural history with a rich and enthralling description of the landscape. He wrote how monkeys filled the jungle with 'melancholy howlings', he wrote how in the mists created by the rapids of the Orinoco 'rainbows danced in a game of hide-and-seek', and he wrote how strange tropical insects 'poured their red phosphoric light on the herb-covered ground which glowed with living fire'. Humboldt created a seductive new genre of nature writing that eloquently described nature as part of the web of life.

Like many others, Darwin was entranced by his work and dreamed of following in his footsteps. He was so excited by Humboldt's description of the island of Tenerife that he decided to organise his own expedition to the island. The plan was for Darwin and a few friends from Cambridge to sail to Tenerife in their summer holidays and spend three weeks botanising and geologising there. He started studying Spanish and spent his free time 'working like a tiger on geology', a subject that during his lectures in Edinburgh he found so boring that he resolved to 'never read a book on geology again'.

It was John Henslow who introduced Darwin to Reverend Adam Sedgwick, the Professor of Geology at Cambridge and who encouraged him to spend the summer on a field trip to Wales studying rock formations and working on a geological map of the countryside:

> Professor Sedgwick in the beginning of August intended to visit North Wales to pursue his famous geological investigation amongst the older rocks ... The tour was of decided use in teaching me a little how to make out the geology of a country. Sedgwick often sent me on a line parallel to his, telling me to bring

back specimens of rocks and to mark the stratification on a map. I have little doubt that he did this for my own good, as I was too ignorant to have aided him.

Darwin returned home to Shrewsbury from his geological excursion in Wales when he found two letters waiting for him which would be completely life-changing. The first letter was in John Henslow's familiar handwriting:

> Cambridge, 24 August 1831
> My Dear Darwin,
> ... I shall hope to see you shortly, fully expecting that you will eagerly catch at the offer which is likely to be made you of a trip to Tierra del Fuego, and home by the East Indies. I have been asked by Peacock ... to recommend him a naturalist as companion to Captain FitzRoy, employed by the government to survey the southern extremity of America. I have stated that I consider you to be the best qualified person I know of who is likely to undertake such a situation ... Captain FitzRoy wants a man (I understand) more as a companion than a mere collector, and would not take anyone, however good a naturalist, who was not recommended to him likewise as a 'gentleman'.
> J.S.Henslow
> The expedition is to sail on 25th September (at earliest) so there is no time to be lost.

The second was a covering letter from one of Henslow's colleagues, the mathematician George Peacock, who was a great friend of Captain Robert FitzRoy:

My Dear Sir,

I received Henslow's letter last night too late to forward it to you by the post; a circumstance which I do not regret, as it has given me the opportunity of seeing Captain Beaufort at the Admiralty (the Hydrographer), and of stating to him the offer which I have to make to you. He entirely approves of it, and you may consider the situation as at your absolute disposal ... Captain FitzRoy (a nephew of the Duke of Grafton) sails at the end of September, in a ship to survey, in the first instance, the South Coast of Tierra del Fuego, afterwards to visit the South Sea Islands, and return by the Indian Archipelago to England ...The ship sails about the end of September, and you must lose no time in making known your acceptance to Captain Beaufort.

Very Truly Yours,
George Peacock

Several Spanish colonies in South America, including Argentina, Chile and Peru, had fought and won their freedom from Spain in 1814 to 1824. Britain, now the world's most powerful maritime nation, wished to gain influence in the region and had established naval stations in Argentina, Brazil and Chile. The existing nautical charts of the coastlines were less than accurate, and in 1826, the British Admiralty sent *HMS Beagle* and its support ship *HMS Adventure* to survey the coastlines around Patagonia and Tierra del Fuego.

A captain in the Royal Navy had to exercise unquestioned power, enforced by severe corporal punishment. He could not afford to become intimate with his officers and crew, however much he might like or respect them, which included eating around a common table. Conversation around the act of breaking bread with our fellow humans is one thing that can help keep us sane, yet the captain usually dined alone. In this first voyage of the *Beagle,* its Captain Pringle Stokes, after two years of stressful and dangerous work, became increasingly depressed and in June 1828 he prophetically wrote in his journal:

Nothing could be more dreary than the scene around us. The lofty, bleak, and barren heights that surround the inhospitable shores of this inlet, were covered, even low down their sides, with dense clouds, upon which the fierce squalls that assailed us beat, without causing any change... Around us, and some of them distant no more than two-thirds of a cable's length, were rocky inlets, lashed by a tremendous surf; and, as if to complete the dreariness and utter desolation of the scene, even the birds seemed to shun its neighborhood. The weather was that in which... the soul of man dies in him.

Overwhelmed by the challenges of the survey and the unforgiving sea conditions, he fell into a deep depression in the desolate waters of Tierra del Fuego. At Port Famine in the Strait of Magellan, he locked himself into his cabin for fourteen days before shooting himself in the head. It was Robert FitzRoy who replaced Captain Pringle Stokes after his long and horrible suicide in the cold and lonely waters off the southern tip of the South American mainland.

In the tragic case of Pringle Stokes the absence of fellowship may have helped cause his suicide. For this reason, Robert FitzRoy felt it was necessary to have a companion on board with whom he could share his meals, his interests and if necessary his worries. Since the voyage was also a scientific one, he sought to find a scientist and a gentleman who, without shipboard duties, could fulfil the role as a companion. In FitzRoy's own words:

> Anxious that no opportunity of collecting useful information, during the voyage, should be lost: I proposed to the Hydrographer that some well-educated and scientific person should be sought for who would willingly share such accommodations as I had to offer, in order to profit by the opportunity of visiting distant countries yet little known. Captain Beaufort

approved of the suggestion, and wrote to Professor Peacock, of Cambridge, who consulted with a friend, Professor Henslow, and he named Mr. Charles Darwin, grandson of Darwin the poet, as a young man of promising ability, extremely fond of geology, and indeed all branches of natural history.

Portrait of Captain Robert FitzRoy
The Narrative of the Voyage of the Beagle, **Wellcome Library**

Darwin was told the voyage would last two years, perhaps even three or four, but he would be free to leave the ship and return home if he found this necessary. He would also be free to go ashore, to explore and collect natural history specimens while the *Beagle* was mapping and doing its hydrographic studies along the coastline. This was the opportunity of a lifetime, a chance to follow his hero Humboldt, to combine exotic travel with scientific discovery, not just in South America but around the entire world, and for the young twenty two year old Charles Darwin there was only one possible response.

But his father was less than enthusiastic. Charles had frittered away his time at Cambridge and now had come up with some foolhardy idea to voyage around the world as a naturalist, something for which he had few academic qualifications. After a difficult conversation with his father, Charles Darwin was obliged to write the following response to John Henslow:

> Shrewesbury, Tuesday [30 August 1831]
> My Dear Sir,
> Mr Peacock's letter arrived on Saturday, 27th and I received it late yesterday evening. As far as my own mind is concerned. I should, I think 'certainly', most gladly have accepted the opportunity which you have so kindly offered me. But my father, although he does not decidedly refuse me, gives me strong advice against going, that I should not be comfortable if I did not follow it ... but if it had not been for my father, I would have taken all risks ... Again I must thank you; it adds a little to the heavy, but pleasant load of gratitude which I owe you.
> CH. Darwin

In the meantime, Robert Darwin probably received counsel from his daughters, who knew how their brother was absolutely shattered by not being able to grasp this opportunity. Having second thoughts, Robert Darwin advised his son that 'If you can find any man of commonsense who advises you to go then I will give my consent' and he gave Darwin a note to take to his uncle, Joshua Wedgwood:

> Charles will tell you of the offer he has had made to him of going for a voyage of discovery for 2 years, - I strongly object to it on various grounds, but I will not detail my reasons that he may have your unbiased opinion on the subject, and if you think differently from me I shall wish him to follow your advice.

Fortunately, his uncle (and future father-in-law) thought it would do Charles no harm as a clergyman and gentleman to have this experience and it might even make a man of him. Joshua Wedgwood asked Charles to write out a list of his father's objections so that he could respond to them one by one. Prompting Charles to write this letter to his father:

> My Dear Father,
> I am afraid I am going to make you again very uncomfortable but upon consideration I think you will excuse me once again stating my opinions on the offer of this voyage. My excuse and reason is in the different way the Wedgwoods view the subject from what you and my sisters do. I have given Uncle Jos, what I hope is an accurate and full list of your objections and he is kind enough to give his opinions on all. The list and his answers will be enclosed. But may I beg you one favour, it will be doing me great kindness, if you will send me a decided answer, yes or no? If the latter, I should be most ungrateful if I did not implicitly yield to your better judgement, and to the kindest indulgence you have shown me all through my life; and you may rely upon it I will never mention the subject again.
> Your affectionate son,
> Charles Darwin

The letters went off in a carriage the next morning and later that day Darwin and his uncle, Joshua Wedgwood travelled to Shrewsbury. By the time they arrived his father had read their letters and had decided to withdraw his opposition. Having formally refused the invitation, was it now too late for Charles to accept? He was up at three a.m. in the morning to catch the express coach to London and try and overtake his letter declining the invitation. He penned this letter to John Henslow later that same night:

> My Dear Sir,
> I am just arrived; you will guess the reason. My father has changed his mind. I trust the place is not given away. I am very much fatigued and am going to bed. I dare say you have not yet got my second letter. How soon shall I come to you in the morning?
> Send a verbal answer.
> Good Night,
> Yours
> C.Darwin

He spent the next few days with Professor Henslow, who explained that an invitation from the Admiralty to join a voyage to Tierra del Fuego had circulated across a number of Cambridge desks before he had put Darwin's name forward for the position. Darwin then returned to London to formally meet with Captain FitzRoy at the Admiralty. Fortunately, the twenty six year old highly experienced Captain and the twenty two year old inexperienced Darwin found themselves compatible. Exalted, barely able to contain his excitement, Darwin quickly wrote a message home to his sister Susan:

> Captain FitzRoy is [in] town, and I have seen him; it is no use trying to praise him as much as I feel inclined to do, for you would not believe me. One thing I am certain, nothing could be more open and kind than he was to me ... We stop for a week at [the] Madeira Islands, and shall see most of [the] big cities in South America. Captain Beaufort is drawing up the track through the South Sea ... There is indeed a tide of affairs in man, and I have experienced it, and I had entirely given it up till today.

6

Charles Darwin - The Voyage of the Beagle

In December 1831, the *Beagle* sailed from England in a voyage that would circumnavigate the world and last nearly five years. This Royal Naval vessel was a hardworking 10-gun brig, 90 feet in length, and with a crew of 65 men commanded by Captain Robert FitzRoy. The object of the voyage was to complete the survey of the coastlines of Patagonia and Tierra del Fuego undertaken during the first voyage of the *Beagle* from 1826 to 1830 and to survey the coastlines of Chile and Peru. The *Beagle* was also ordered to circumnavigate the world and measure an unbroken chain of times and thus longitudes at specific ports around the globe using the Royal Observatory at Greenwich as a reference point. The invention of an accurate marine clock by John Harrison allowed the measurement of local time compared to another clock measuring the time at Greenwich. Since the earth revolves 360 degrees of longitude in 24 hours, the time difference can be used to calculate longitude at any point on the globe. Harrison's marine chronometer revolutionised navigation and greatly increased the safety of sea travel. Different watchmakers had tried making his chronometer, and for this voyage, the *Beagle* was equipped with twenty-two marine chronometers to test their efficiency and reliability in their long voyage around the world. Sixteen were provided by the Admiralty, and in his pursuit of absolute efficiency, Robert FitzRoy provided another six at his own expense. FitzRoy employed an instrument maker, George James Stebbing, to look after the chronometers; his only job was to ensure they were regularly and properly wound, and no one else was allowed into the chronometer room. No vessel had been better equipped with a set of chronometers than the *Beagle*, and Captain FitzRoy was able to write in his final report to the Admiralty that he had established a connected chain of meridian distances around the globe, the first time this had ever been accomplished by means of chronometers alone.

Robert FitzRoy was born into the upper echelons of the British aristocracy and their tradition of public service. Through his father, General Lord Charles FitzRoy, Robert was a fourth great-grandson of Charles II of England. He entered the Royal Navy College at the age of twelve and first went to sea at the age of fourteen. When eighteen, he was promoted to lieutenant after passing the examination with 'full numbers' (100%) and was the first to achieve this result. As the imperious aristocrat that he was, he saw the world in black and white, right and wrong, and there were no shades in between. Only twenty-six years old when given the command of the *Beagle*, he was immensely qualified but ruled his ship with an iron fist. Considered to be at his worst in the mornings, when he made his inspections of the ship and its crew, he was generally able to detect something amiss and was unsparing in his blame. The junior officers, when they relieved each other, would ask 'whether much hot coffee had been served out this morning?' meaning how was the captain's temper? FitzRoy was deeply religious, as the Church was an integral part of the aristocratic world to which he belonged. He believed in the literal truth of the Bible and thought the voyage would provide someone like Charles Darwin a great opportunity to find evidence of the first appearance of all God's creatures on earth and of the Biblical Flood.

Bad weather delayed the departure of the *Beagle,* and they were still in harbour on Christmas Day. For some of the crew, it might be the last Christmas in England they would ever see, so they decided to make it a memorable one, and some returned to the ship, late, drunk and insolent. The next day, many men were unfit for duty and were placed in irons. As Darwin noted in his diary, 'the ship has been all day in a state of anarchy ... Several have paid the penalty for insolence, by sitting for eight or nine hours in heavy chains'. This was going to be a long voyage and FitzRoy was unflinching in providing the naval discipline required, as he recorded in his log:

> John Bruce: 25 lashes for drunkenness, quarrelling and insolence.
> David Russel: 34 lashes for breaking his leave and disobeying orders.
> James Phipps: 44 lashes for breaking his leave, drunkenness and insolence.
> Elias Davis: 31 lashes for reported neglect of duty.

For the pampered and privileged Charles Darwin, the sounds of the lash and the screams of suffering would have been a harsh introduction to Navy life - yet his own diary remains strangely silent on this matter. The early weeks at sea were a misery for Darwin as he suffered severely from sea-sickness, a problem which was to continue for the rest of the voyage. He wrote to his family that:

> The misery I endured is far beyond what I ever guessed at ... The real misery only begins when you are so exhausted that a little exertion makes a feeling of faintness come on – I found that nothing but lying in a hammock did any good.

In the small poop cabin he shared with two other crew members, his hammock was strung above the table where the ship's officers updated their sea charts, so there was no room for privacy. On a small shelf next to his hammock were Darwin's most precious possessions, a copy of the *Personal Narrative of a Journey to the Equinoctial Regions of the New Continent* by Alexander von Humboldt and the *Principles of Geology* by Charles Lyell. It was Humboldt who reasoned that a glimpse into God's divine plan could be achieved by the comparison of one botanical region with another and the English translation of his work excited Darwin to emulate his scientist hero as he wrote:

> My admiration of his famous personal narrative (part of which I almost know by heart) determined me to travel in distant countries, and led me to volunteer as a naturalist in her Majesty's ship *Beagle*.

Humboldt believed that the naturalist's task was to discover both the diversity and the underlying unity of nature and 'the naturalist should aim to collect, classify, measure and map the whole natural order.' Darwin had been so excited by Humboldt's description of the island of Tenerife that he had planned to organise an expedition to the island himself. Unfortunately for Darwin, the *Beagle* and its crew had to leave the tropical paradise of Tenerife without landing because of cholera-related quarantine restrictions.

One of the great ironies in the history of science is that before they left England, it was Robert FitzRoy who gave Darwin a copy of the first volume of Charles Lyell's *Principles of Geology*, which had only just been published. Darwin arranged for the remaining volumes to be sent to him and received the second volume when he was in Montevideo. These books taught Darwin how to understand the earth in the same language as it is currently written in, that is, by understanding current landforms and current geological processes such as erosion, deposition of sediments, glaciation and volcanism. Lyell claimed that from his studies of the fossil record, the earth was millions of years in the making, rather than the six thousand years claimed by theologians. (It was in 1650 that the Archbishop James Ussher calculated that the Creation as described in the Book of Genesis had occurred on October 22, 4004 BC and was completed six days later).

Lyell wrote that rather than the earth being shaped by cataclysmic events such as the biblical Flood, it was the natural processes of erosion by rain, wind and waves followed by sedimentation and then uplift, repeated over many millions of years, which had shaped the earth's surface and his book was subtitled *An Attempt to Explain the Former Changes of the Earth's Surface, by Reference to Causes Now in Operation*. However, Lyell did not extend his theories from the world of rocks to the organic world. Even in the face of his own evidence against it, he clung to the idea of a Creationist God who would have to be constantly restocking the world with new species, different but similar to those which had just been destroyed by some geological catastrophe. His doctrine of small accumulative changes soon became the underlying principle of Darwin's geological studies, 'It altered the whole tone of one's mind, and therefore ... when seeing a thing never seen by Lyell, one yet saw it partially through his eyes'. Inspired by Charles Lyell, the young Darwin began his geological studies at Porto Praya in the Cape Verde Islands, and you can sense his excitement in describing this geological outcrop:

> The geology of this island is the most interesting part of its natural history. On entering the harbour, a perfectly horizontal white band, in the face of the sea cliff, may be seen running for some miles along the coast, and at the height of about forty-five feet above the water. Upon examination, this white stratum is found to consist of calcareous matter with numerous shells embedded, most or all of which now exist on the neighbouring coast. It rests on ancient volcanic rocks and has been covered by a stream of basalt, which must have entered the sea when the white shelly bed was lying at the bottom.

Here was geology in action. The basalt had flowed out from an associated volcano to cover the shell beds on the sea floor, the island had then been slowly pushed up by subterranean forces, and the irregularities in the white band indicated these forces were still in action. Fifty years later, Darwin still remembered the impact of this day and when it first dawned on him that he might write a book on the geology of the various countries he was going to visit, and how this idea made him thrill with delight. At the end of February, the *Beagle* reached the coast of South America at San Salvador in Brazil. Here, Darwin was able to explore a tropical forest for the first time, another day that he will obviously never forget:

> The day has passed delightfully. Delight itself, however, is a weak term to express the feelings of a naturalist who, for the first time, has wandered by himself in a Brazilian forest. The elegance of the grasses, the novelty of the parasitical plants, the beauty of the flowers, the glossy green of the foliage, but above all the general luxuriance of the vegetation, filled me with admiration. A most paradoxical mixture of sound and silence pervades the shady parts of the wood. The noise from the insects is so loud that it may be heard even in a vessel anchored several hundred yards from the shore; yet within the recesses of the forest a universal silence appears to reign. To a person fond of natural history, such a day as this brings with it a deeper pleasure than he can ever hope to experience again.

It was at San Salvador that Darwin described a disagreement with Robert FitzRoy. The Darwin and the Wedgewood families were staunch abolitionists, and both his grandfathers had played a prominent role in the anti-slavery movement. While in San Salvador, Darwin found the sights of slavery offensive, and when FitzRoy defended the practice by describing a recent visit to a slave owner whose slaves replied "no" on being asked by their master if they wished to be freed,

Darwin suggested that answers in such circumstances were worthless. Enraged that his word had been questioned, FitzRoy lost his temper and banned Darwin from his company. Darwin thought that he would have to leave the ship, but within hours, FitzRoy sent an apology and asked Darwin to return. In his autobiography, Darwin wrote of FitzRoy that he was extremely kind to him, but the difficulty of living on good terms with a Captain of a Man-of-War is much increased by it being almost mutinous to answer him as one would answer anyone else.

Throughout the voyage, Darwin gathered plants, birds, rocks and marine creatures, and it was from Rio de Janeiro that he sent back his first shipment to England for later description and assessment. During his stay here, Darwin resided in a cottage in the beautiful Botofogo Bay just below the well-known Corcovado Mountain, upon which now stands the famous statue of *Christ the Redeemer*. From here, he made collecting excursions into the countryside or visited the Botanic Gardens where the leaves of the camphor, pepper, cinnamon and clove trees were delightfully aromatic, while the breadfruit, jackfruit and mango trees vied with each other in the magnificence of their foliage. Sitting outside his house in the cool of the tropical evening, he would delight in the great concert provided by the natural world as frogs, cicadas, and crickets ceaselessly called to each other.

From Rio de Janeiro the *Beagle* sailed south to Montevideo and then to the Rio Negro. It was in Montevideo that the ship's artist Augustus Earle fell ill and it was here that Robert FitzRoy engaged Conrad Martens as a draughtsman to replace him. One of Darwin's most significant discoveries was at Punta Alta, the high cliffs overlooking the harbour of Bahia Blanca. Here, the fossil remains of nine great quadrupeds and many detached bones were found in the cliffs along the beach. These were the bones of the giant megafauna which had previously roamed these plains and later described as *Megatherium* (a giant sloth), *Megalonyx*, *Scelidotherium*, *Mylodon* and *Toxodon* (a giant capybara type rodent) and *Glyptodon* (a giant type of armadillo). The teeth of these animals indicate they were vegetarians and fed off the grasses and leaves that existed in the area. Darwin describes his discovery:

> I obtained a jaw bone, which contained a tooth: by this I found that it belongs to the great ante-diluvia animal the Megatherium (like a giant sloth). This is particularly interesting as the only specimens in Europe are in the King's collection at Madrid, where for all purposes of science they are nearly as well hidden as if in their primeval rock.

These giant bones were the remains of extinct animals, and extinct animals were supposed to bear no ancestral relationship to living species. However, Darwin recognised they were similar to species now living in the same area, such as the tree-climbing sloths, the burrowing armadillo and the rodent-like guanaco. Had these giant beasts died out in the Biblical Flood and then been replaced by the animals that Noah took on his Ark? Or could they be linked by descent? Was it an example of what was then called transmutation - considered a wild idea espoused only by a few followers of the French naturalist Jean-Baptiste Lamarck? These were questions that went directly to the origin of species, questions which the young Darwin knew were important, but which he was still unable to answer:

> This wonderful relationship in the same continent between the dead and the living, will, I do not doubt, hereafter throw more light on the appearance of organic beings on our earth, and their disappearance from it, than any other class of facts.

Towards the end of July, the *Beagle* reached the east coast of modern Argentina, where its crew began the laborious task of survey triangulations up and down the east coast for the next year. The coastline was mapped using a compass, a sextant to calculate latitude, and the ship's twenty-two chronometers to calculate longitude. Soundings were taken to map water depth, shoals and reefs, and records were kept of the currents, tides, winds and other natural hazards. As described by Robert FitzRoy:

> Our first object was to find a safe harbour in which to secure the ship. There we made observations of latitude, time and true bearing; on tides and magnetism. We also made a plan of the harbour and its environs; and triangulations, including all the visible heights, and more remarkable features of the coast, so far as it could be clearly distinguished from the summits of the highest hills near the harbour. Upon these summits a good theodolite was used.

The months the *Beagle* spent surveying coastlines allowed Darwin ample time to spend ashore collecting insects, beetles, butterflies, birds, plants, rocks and fossils. September 1832 found him galloping on horseback across the Argentinian pampas 'shooting, riding, collecting and looking forward to a few revolutions'. As there was a standing order aboard the ship forbidding land excursions alone, Darwin was accompanied by his assistant Syms Covington, who originally signed aboard as 'fiddler and boy to the poop cabin'. He was now on Darwin's payroll and he taught him to shoot, collect, preserve and pack specimens. Syms Covington remained a good friend and in the employ of Charles Darwin after they returned to London and until he migrated to Australia in 1839.

From Carmen de Patagones at the mouth of the Rio Negro, Darwin undertook a long overland journey of 960 kilometres back to Buenos Aires and subsequently another 960 kilometre journey up the Parana River from Buenos Aires to Santa Fe and back. Darwin revelled in these journeys, travelling on the open plains, hunting for deer and ostriches, living with the gauchos, meeting with the armies of General Rosas who were putting down an Indian revolt, and in his diary he writes of the pleasure of living in the open air – 'with the sky for a roof and the ground for a table'. During his excursions across the Argentinian pampas, Darwin seems to regularly find, or is regularly directed to, outcrops containing the fossilised bones of animals, many of which are extinct, but are also related to existing species:

> It is impossible to reflect on the changed state of the American continent without the deepest astonishment. Formerly it must have swarmed with great monsters: now we find mere pygmies, compared with the antecedent, allied races ... What, then, has exterminated so many species and whole genera? The mind at first is irresistibly hurried into the belief of some great catastrophe; but thus to destroy animals, large and small in both South and North America, we must shake the entire framework of the globe ... Certainly, no fact in the long history of the world is so startling as the wide and repeated exterminations of its inhabitants'.

Travelling the plains, Darwin saw many examples of the rhea or South American version of the ostrich, which were hunted for food by Gauchos using their twirling *bolas*, which are thrown around the rhea's legs to render them immobile. The large rhea is abundant on the northern plains of Argentina, but it is the smaller rhea that is more abundant in the south. It was in Patagonia that his crew shot a small rhea and it went into the cooking pot. It was half-eaten before Darwin realised it was a new species that he wanted for his collection, the bones were quickly pieced together and the animal was subsequently named *Rhea darwinii* in his honour.

During that first voyage of the *Beagle*, Robert FitzRoy had taken four Fuegian natives hostage after the ship's whaleboat had been stolen while in Tierra del Fuego. The boat was never recovered and FitzRoy then had to decide what to do with the three men and a young girl, and he wrote:

> I began to think of various advantages which might result to them and their countrymen, as well as to us, by taking them to England, educating them there as far as might be practicable, and then bringing them back to Tierra del Fuego.

In England, the Church Missionary Society provided the Fuegians with accommodation and education at an infant school, which provided a rudimentary education in English, Christianity, the use of common tools, care of farm animals, and gardening. One of the men died following his smallpox vaccination, but FitzRoy was committed to his promise to return the remaining three Fuegians to their native lands in Tierra del Fuego. It was FitzRoy's hope that these 'civilised' Fuegians whom he had named Jemmy Button, York Minster and Fuegia Basket would, together with a young English missionary, Mr Mathews, establish a Mission and bring a civilising influence to the wilds of Patagonia. Here, the natives lived on shellfish and what fish or seals they could catch. Their bodies are quite naked, although smeared with grease and covered with guanaco cloaks or sealskins to keep them warm. Darwin's first sight of the wild Fuegians shocked him immensely, and he wrote that viewing such men, their faces daubed with white paint, their hair entangled, their skins filthy and greasy, he could hardly make himself believe they were fellow creatures. This striking comparison would have given Darwin many hours of thought about the ascent of man from savagery to civilisation:

> It was without exception the most curious and interesting spectacle I ever beheld. I could not have believed how wide is the difference between savage and civilized man, it is greater

than between a wild and domesticated animal, in as much as in man there is a greater power of improvement.

The crew of the *Beagle* helped set up a Mission post in the Beagle Channel with huts, gardens, furniture and crockery, and left Mr Mathews and the three Fuegians to bring the benefits of civilisation to Tierra del Fuego. Unfortunately, when the *Beagle* returned from their surveying it was obvious their civilising experiment had failed. The Mission post had been looted and its possessions divided up amongst the natives. Mathews, who was in fear of his life, chose to rejoin the ship; the three Fuegians had reverted to their native habits, and Jemmy Button was now quite naked except for a rag around his waist. FitzRoy must have been disappointed that his attempt at civilising the Fuegians had failed.

**Chart of the Beagle Channel by *HMS Beagle*, 1834
showing Darwin Sound and Mount Darwin**

The Beagle Channel, which provides a link between the Atlantic and the Pacific Oceans, is 240 kilometres long and only about five kilometres wide at its narrowest point. The shoreline is covered in dense forest, and on the north side, there is a range of mountains beginning with Mount Darwin and culminating in Mount Sarmiento, which are covered in perpetual snow. Glaciers extend from the mountains down to the water's edge, and Darwin wrote in his field notes that 'It is scarcely possible to imagine anything more beautiful than the beryl-like blue of these glaciers, especially as contrasted with the dead white of the upper expanse of snow'.

HMS Beagle, the Beagle Channel and Mount Sarmiento, Conrad Martens

In May 1834, the *Beagle* cleared Tierra del Fuego to enter the Pacific Ocean and headed north to Valparaiso, where it began its hydrographic surveys up and down the west coast of South America. While anchored off the island of Chiloe, they observed the snow-covered cone of the Orsono volcano spewing huge volumes of ash and smoke, and Darwin describes the erupting volcano:

> At midnight the sentry observed something like a large star, which gradually increased in size till about three o'clock, when it presented a magnificent spectacle. By the aid of a glass, dark objects, in constant succession, were seen, in the midst of a great glare of red light, to be thrown up and fall down. The light was sufficient to cast on the water a long bright reflection.

One month later, while he was resting in a wood outside Valdivia, Darwin felt the ground shake. Leaping to his feet, he had no difficulty standing upright, but the motion made him giddy, and he wrote:

> A bad earthquake at once destroys our oldest associations: the earth, the very emblem of solidity, has moved beneath our feet like a thin crust over a fluid – one second of time has created in the mind a strange idea of insecurity which hours of reflection would not have produced ... and in seeing the laboured works of man in a moment overthrown, we feel the insignificance of his boasted power.

Darwin was standing near the junction where the Nazca oceanic plate slides gradually beneath the western edge of the continental South American plate, causing the uplift of the Andes Mountains and volcanic eruptions down the west coast of South America. The South American continental plate was on the move and arriving in the harbour of Concepcion, the crew of the *Beagle* found that not a house was left standing, as the tsunami wave generated by the earthquake had washed them away, and the coast was strewn with timber and furniture. Darwin saw the human tragedy of the collapsed homes and the smashed buildings caused by the earthquake, but significantly, he observed how these geological forces had driven the land higher:

> The most remarkable effect of this earthquake was the permanent elevation of the land, though it would probably be more correct to speak of it as the cause. There can be no doubt that the land round the Bay of Concepcion was raised two or three feet ... and at the island of San Maria (about thirty miles distant) the elevation was greater; on one part, Captain FitzRoy found beds of putrid mussel shells still adhering to the rocks ten feet above high water mark ... At Valparaiso, as I have remarked, similar shells are found at the height of 1300 feet: it is hardly possible to doubt that this great elevation has been effected by successive small uprisings, such as that which accompanied or caused the earthquake of this year, and likewise by an insensibly slow rise, which is certainly in progress on some parts of this coast.

From Santiago, Darwin embarked on a twenty-four-day expedition east across the Andes towards Mendoza before returning to Valparaiso. Reaching a village outside Santiago, where there were several pretty senoritas, he describes how they were horrified at him entering a church without first praying, asking him, "Why do you not become a Christian – for our religion is certain"? He assured them he was a sort of Christian (of the Anglican sort?). They then asked him, "Do not your padres, your very bishops, marry"? The absurdity of a bishop having a wife particularly struck them, and he describes how they scarcely knew whether to be amused or horror-struck at such an enormity.

Climbing up the western side of the Andes, Darwin was able to apply his Lyellian geological principles on a grand scale and wrote that he could see 'manifest proofs of excessive violence as the strata of the highest pinnacles are tossed about like crusts of a broken pie'. Darwin finally reached the Continental Divide at 4000 metres above sea level, where even his mules had difficulty breathing. He describes the exertion of walking at these high altitudes as great and his breathing as deep and laborious, but the excitement of finding fossil marine shells on the highest ridges of the Andes, surrounded by snow-capped mountains, completely dispelled any fatigue. Feeling on top of the world, he writes poetically of the view from the top of the Andes:

> When we reached the crest and looked backwards, a glorious view was presented. The atmosphere so resplendently clear, the sky an immense blue, the profound valleys, the wild broken forms, the heaps of ruins piled up during the lapse of ages, the bright coloured rocks, contrasted with the quiet mountains of snow, together produced a scene I never could have imagined. Neither a plant nor bird, excepting a few condors wheeling around the higher pinnacles, distracted the attention from the inanimate mass. – I felt glad I was by myself, it was like watching a thunderstorm, or hearing in the full Orchestra a Chorus of the Messiah.

Even for someone like Darwin, finding fossil marine shells, thousands of feet up on the highest ridges of the Andes, was unbelievable. Discussing these observations later with FitzRoy, he was probably met with disbelief if not ridicule, and in writing his narrative of *The Voyage of the Beagle*, he felt the need to be more conservative:

> I have certain proofs that this part of the continent of South America has been elevated near the coast, at least from four hundred to five hundred feet since the epoch of the existing shells, and further inland the rise may have been possibly greater.

Darwin's collecting of flora, fauna and rock samples caused some confusion in South America and he describes an incident in Peru when a villager is asked in conversation what he thought of the King of England sending out someone to Peru to pick up lizards, beetles, and break stones. The villager thinks seriously and then replies, "It is not well. No man is so rich as to send out people to pick up such rubbish. I do not like it: if one of us were to go and do such things in England, do you not think the King of England would very soon send us out of his country?"

FitzRoy had purchased and fitted out a ship in Argentina, which he renamed the *Adventurer,* to help with the surveying and act as a support vessel. This virtually doubled his charting progress and offered his crew some safety in the hazardous waters around Cape Horn and Tierra del Fuego. Hydrographic surveying is hazardous because the survey ship is always sailing close to the coastline and in uncharted waters. At any time, a reef or pinnacle could rise out of the depths and wreck the vessel or a gale could drive them onto a rocky coast. This required constant vigilance by all of the crew and especially the captain. The stress had taken its toll on Pringle Stokes and it was beginning to take its toll on Robert FitzRoy. He knew that his orders from the Admiralty did not include a second vessel and in his letter requesting their approval, he wrote:

> I believe their Lordships will approve of what I have done, but if I am wrong, no inconvenience will result to the public service, since I alone am responsible for the agreement ... and am able and willing to pay the stipulated sum.

FitzRoy saw an additional vessel as essential for the safety of himself and his crew. He certainly hoped for Admiralty approval as this was the first time that a survey vessel had been ordered to operate without a support vessel. Captain Beaufort was supportive and, in his letter of recommendation to the Admiralty, stated that it was unusually risky to send a ship alone to explore a remote corner of the world because if she struck a reef, her crew could easily perish without a support vessel standing by. Thus, FitzRoy was entirely unprepared for the Admiralty's response when their Lordships did not approve of him hiring an additional vessel and desired that it be discharged as soon as possible. There would be no reimbursement and FitzRoy was forced to sell the *Adventure* below his cost. It was a double loss and a blow that affected FitzRoy deeply. Darwin was the closest to him, and during that winter, FitzRoy's depression seemed to be bordering on insanity. In a letter home, Darwin wrote that:

> He had a morbid depression of spirits and had lost all decision and resolution. The Captain was afraid that his mind was becoming deranged.

The suicide of his predecessor on the *Beagle*, Captain Pringle Stokes, must have also weighed heavily on FitzRoy's mind and he decided to resign his command. Lieutenant Wickham was the second-in-charge, but he carefully pointed out to FitzRoy that the instructions from the Admiralty were to survey as much of the southwest coast of South America as possible, not to survey all of it, and that if he were to take command he would sail directly across the Pacific and complete the rest of their planned voyage as soon as possible. After further contemplation and after recovering his strong sense of duty, FitzRoy decided to withdraw his resignation, and the *Beagle* spent another year surveying the west coast of South America before he decided his work was done.

In September 1835, almost four years after leaving England, the *Beagle* sailed north and east into the Pacific Ocean. Their next stop was the Galapagos Islands. Here, the landscape is pock-marked with thousands of small volcanic craters, and almost the entire surface of the islands is covered in lava and associated red scoria. In the distance, Darwin could see smoke and ash being emitted from the summit of one of the larger volcanoes. This was new land being created in the Pacific Ocean 900 kilometres from the South American continent:

> In the morning we landed on Chatham Island, which like the others, rises with a tame and rounded outline broken here

and there by scattered hillocks, the remains of former craters. Nothing could be less inviting than the first appearance. A broken field of black basaltic lava thrown into the most rugged waves, and crossed by great fissures, is everywhere covered by stunted, sunburnt brushwood, which shows little sign of life. The dry and parched surface, being heated by the noon-day sun, gave the air a close and sultry feeling, like that from a stove.

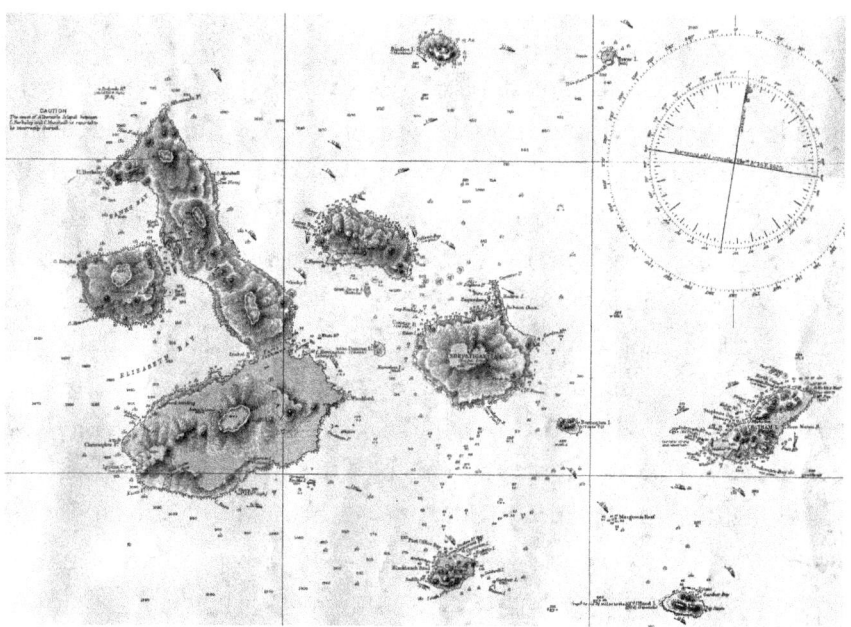

Chart of the Galapagos Islands, HMS Beagle, 1839

This new land was slowly being populated by plants, animals and birds that could only have reached here from South America. Darwin soon realised that he was surrounded by new species of birds and animals which were similar yet different to those he had seen in Chile and Peru:

> The natural history of these islands is eminently curious, and well deserves attention. Most of the organic productions are aboriginal creations found nowhere else; there is even a difference between the inhabitants of different islands; yet all show a marked relationship with those of America, though separated from that continent by an open ocean between 500 and 600 miles in width. The archipelago is a little world within itself, or rather a satellite attached to America, whence it has derived a few stray colonists and received the general character of its indigenous productions.

Darwin also noted the unusual tameness of the creatures on the islands, as if they had not yet developed any fear of man and he wrote, 'A gun here is almost superfluous, for with the muzzle of one I pushed a hawk off the branch of a tree'. On another occasion, a mockingbird landed on top of a water pitcher he was holding and proceeded to drink from it. He describes how he tried and very nearly succeeded in catching birds by their legs. There were also both marine and land-based iguanas on the island. The species are quite distinct in appearance, and the marine iguana is remarkable because it is only found on the Galapagos Islands and is the only known lizard that lives on marine vegetation. Another significant feature of the Galapagos Islands is the giant tortoise which can be found in large numbers on all of the islands:

> I have not yet noted the most remarkable feature in the natural history of the archipelago by far: it is that the different islands to a considerable extent are inhabited by a different set of beings. My attention was first drawn to this fact by the Vice-Governor, Mr Lawson, declaring that the tortoises differed from the different islands and that he could with certainty tell from which island any one was brought.

Darwin also observed how the mockingbirds seemed different from island to island and were also different from those of continental South America. Unfortunately, he was in a hurry to collect as many bird specimens as possible and did not take the time to label each island location accurately. However, the mysteries of the Galapagos Islands were to remain on Darwin's mind, and he wrote in his diary:

> Considering the small size of the islands, we feel the more astonished at the number of their aboriginal beings, and at their confined range. Seeing every height crowned with its crater, and the boundaries of most of the lava streams still distinct, we are led to believe that within a period of geologically recent time the unbroken ocean was here spread out. Hence, both in space and time, we seem to be brought somewhere near to that great fact – that mystery of mysteries – the first appearance of new beings on this earth.

7

Charles Darwin - In Australia

It was now time for the *Beagle* to cross the vast Pacific Ocean towards Australia. Until now, Darwin had spent more time on his expeditions around South America than he had spent on the *Beagle,* and this long voyage would remind him how he had never gained his 'sea-legs'. Continuing to suffer from sea-sickness, he wrote some advice to would-be voyagers:

> If a person suffers much from seasickness, let him weigh it heavily in the balance. I speak from experience: it is no trifling evil cured in a week ... it must be borne in mind how large a proportion of the time, during a long voyage, is spent on the water, as compared to the days in harbour. And what of the boasted glories of the illimitable ocean? A tedious waste, a desert of water, as the Arabian calls it ... On a forlorn and weather-beaten coast, the scene is indeed different, but the feelings partake more of horror than wild delight.

With only his notes and his reading to keep him occupied while sailing across the blue ocean, or 'tedious waste' as he described it, he had plenty of time to think of home and loved ones from whom he had now been away for almost four years. Already a year longer than previously planned, and the *Beagle* was still only halfway around the world. All on board were looking forward to Sydney and in their imagination saw it as a little England and 'their home away from home'. In writing to his sister, Darwin said:

> For the last year I have been wishing to return and have uttered my wishes in no gentle murmurs; but now I feel inclined to keep up one steady growl from morning to night ... there is no more geology, but plenty of seasickness ... I am looking forward to seeing Sydney, than to any other part of the voyage – our stay here will be very short, only a fortnight; I hope however to be able to take a ride some way into the country.

Darwin's first view of Sydney was disappointing. As the *Beagle* approached Sydney Heads in January 1836, instead of beholding a verdant country interspersed with fine houses, the line of yellowish cliffs reminded him of the coast of Patagonia. Only a solitary lighthouse, built of white stone, told them they were near a great and populous city. Entering the harbour, the shores of horizontally stratified sandstone lined with thin, scrubby trees immediately told him of the country's sterility. He could only write that the country looked a little like England after reaching Sydney Cove and seeing it filled with large sailing ships, surrounded by warehouses, two and three story stone houses and nice cottages. In a letter to his sister Susan, he describes his despair after learning there was no mail for the *Beagle*:

> On coming to Anchor I was full of eager expectations; but a damp was soon thrown over the whole scene by the news that there was not a single letter for the *Beagle*, - None of you at home, can imagine what grief this is. There is no help for it: We did not formerly expect to have arrived here so soon, and so

farewell letters. – The same fate will follow us to the Cape of Good Hope and probably when we reach England, I shall not have received a letter dated within the last 18 months. And now that I have told my pitiable story. I feel much inclined to sit down and have a good cry.

**View of Sydney, Augustus Earle, 1826
National Gallery of Australia**

It was Joseph Banks who, in 1779, suggested to a House of Commons committee that Botany Bay would be a suitable site for a penal colony. He is considered one of Australia's founding fathers as Banks and the idea of founding a penal colony at Botany Bay are irrevocably tied together. His continued interest in the colony of New South Wales and its development earned him another title as the 'Minister for New South Wales'. The First Fleet arrived in January 1788 with two Royal Navy vessels, three store ships, and six convict transports carrying around 750 convicts (550 male and 200 female), with 245 marines plus 50 of their wives and children, and a vast quantity of stores. Unfortunately, Governor Phillip's plan to bring skilled tradesmen to the proposed colony had been rejected. Amazingly, no gardeners, botanists or farmers were sent to help establish the colony, and it makes one wonder how they were expected to survive in this barren land. They soon realised that Botany Bay did not live up to the glowing accounts that Sir Joseph Banks had provided. The bay was open and unprotected, the water was too shallow to allow the ships to anchor close to the shore, fresh water was scarce, and the soil was poor. The First Fleet Commander and Governor-designate, Captain Arthur Phillip, departed Botany Bay in three small boats to explore other bays to the north. Phillip discovered that Port Jackson, about 12 kilometres to the north, was an excellent site for a colony with sheltered anchorages, fresh water and access to more fertile soil along the Parramatta River:

> Governor Phillip had the satisfaction to find one of the finest harbours in the world, in which a thousand sail of the line might ride in perfect security. The different coves of this harbour were examined with all possible expedition, and the preference was given to one which had the finest spring of water, and in which ships can anchor so close to the shore, that at a very small expense, quays may be constructed at which the largest vessels may unload. This cove is about half a mile in length, and a quarter of a mile across at the entrance. In honour of Lord Sydney, the Governor distinguished it by the name of Sydney Cove.

Lord Sydney had made a fundamental decision about the settlement that was to influence it from the start. Instead of just establishing it as a military prison, he provided for a civil administration, with courts of law. For example, after their arrival, two convicts, Henry and Susannah Kable, sought to sue Duncan Sinclair, the captain of their transport ship, for stealing their possessions during the voyage. Convicts in Britain had no right to sue, and Sinclair had boasted that he could not be sued by them. Despite this, the new court found for the plaintiffs and ordered the captain to make restitution for the loss of their possessions. The early days of the settlement were chaotic and difficult. With limited supplies, the cultivation of food was imperative, but the soils around Sydney were poor, the climate was unfamiliar, and very few of the convicts had any knowledge of agriculture. The penal colony was on the verge of outright starvation for extended periods and had to send ships to Cape Town and Batavia for supplies. The marines, poorly disciplined themselves, did not appear interested in imposing any discipline other than the lash on the convicts. Arthur Phillip had to appoint overseers from among the ranks of the convicts to get the others working, and this was the beginning of the process of convict emancipation.

When Charles Darwin and the *Beagle* arrived, only fifty years later, the colony now consisted of 23,000 people, including convicts still serving their term of transportation, emancipists (freed convicts), free settlers and the troops of the New South Wales Corps. Darwin went ashore to explore the town and was impressed by the prosperity of the settlement. He noted how a man of business, often an ex-convict, could hardly fail to make a large fortune as a hotel licensee, shopkeeper or property speculator:

> In the evening I walked through the town and returned full of admiration at the whole scene – It is the most magnificent testimony of the power of the British nation – My first feeling was to congratulate myself, that I was born an Englishman – Upon seeing more of the town on other days, perhaps it fell a little in my estimation; but yet it is a good town; the streets are regular, broad, clean and kept in excellent order; the houses are of a good size and the shops excellent.

Darwin was surprised at the number of large houses just finished and the number of new houses being built, yet everyone complained of the high rents and the difficulty in procuring a house. Those currently living in Sydney, almost two hundred years later, will readily concur with this fact. Darwin took the opportunity to call on his friend and shipmate, Conrad Martens, who had left the *Beagle* in Valparaiso and travelled to Sydney on another vessel. Here he had established a studio on Bridge Street and quickly became one of the leading artists in the colony. Both Darwin and FitzRoy visited his studio to greet him and purchased paintings Martens had made of the *Beagle* during its voyages around South America.

The *Beagle* was only going to be in Sydney for two weeks to resupply and compare the longitude from their chronometers with the longitude previously calculated for the Sydney Observatory. Darwin wished to see as much of Australia as possible and make his own collections of its unique flora and fauna. After only three days in town, he hired a man and two horses to take him to Bathurst, which was 190 kilometres into the interior and an expanding pastoral centre. On the road from Sydney to Parramatta, he saw chain gangs of convicts working on public projects, which he found an unsettling sight, but it also explained the rapid progress of the Colony:

> The most novel and not very pleasing object are the Iron gangs; or parties of Convicts, who have committed some trifling offence in this country; they are generally dressed in yellow and grey clothes, and working in Irons on the roads; they are guarded by sentries with loaded arms - I believe one great means of the early prosperity of these Colonies is Government thus being able to send large parties at once to make good means of communication nearer the Settlers.

Darwin spent the night at what he considered a very comfortable Inn at Emu Ferry, on the banks of the Nepean River and about 55 kilometres west of Sydney. He describes the trees during his journey as being nearly all eucalypts belonging to the one family, with their foliage being scanty, mostly placed in a vertical position and of a particular pale green tint without any gloss. January is the middle of the Australian summer. It was hot, dry, dusty, and in contrast to the forests of South America, the country seemed arid and sterile:

> Although this is such a flourishing country, the appearance of infertility is to a certain extent the truth; the soil without doubt is good, but there is so great a deficiency in rain and running water that it cannot produce much. The Agricultural crops and indeed those in Gardens, are estimated to fail once in three years; and it has so happened on more than one successive year. So that the Colony cannot supply itself with the bread and vegetables which its inhabitants consume. It is essentially pastoral, and chiefly so for sheep and not the larger animals: the alluvial land near Emu Ferry is some of the best cultivated which I have seen; and certainly the scenery on the banks of the Nepean, bounded to the west by the Blue Mountains, was pleasing even to the eye of a person thinking of England.

The Blue Mountains may have looked impressive as they rose up from the Emu Plains, but once on the sandstone plateau, Darwin found the scenery exceedingly monotonous, with scrubby gum trees lining each side of the road and with little traffic except for the occasional bullock wagon piled high with bales of wool. After reaching Wentworth Falls, he stayed the night at the Weatherboard Inn and the next morning walked down Jamison Creek until the ground fell away beneath him into what he described as a 'grand amphitheatre'. Darwin looked out over a vast valley carved into the plateau with the vertical cliffs of the Sydney sandstone causing Wentworth Falls to drop hundreds of metres towards the floor of the Kedumba River, the terrain all covered in a forest of eucalypts that extended to the horizon. Darwin saw this as an ancient seacoast when in fact the uplift of the Blue Mountains had allowed the ancient Kedumba River to carve out a large valley through the resistant sandstone that forms the cliffs and headlands:

> Suddenly and without any preparation, through the trees, which border the pathway, an immense gulf is seen at a depth of perhaps 1500 feet beneath one's feet. Walking a few yards further, one stands on the brink of a precipice. Below is a grand bay or gulf, for I know not what other name to give it, thickly covered with forest. The point of view is situated as it were at the head of the Bay, for the line of cliff diverges away on each side, showing headland, behind headland, as on a bold sea coast.

View of the Jamison Valley at Wentworth Falls
Conrad Martens
Dixson Collection, State Library of NSW

The same view still exists today as the Blue Mountains Heritage area is the largest protected area of high diversity eucalypts on the continent. More than one million acres of National Park contain 91 different eucalypts, a large number but still only a little more than 10 per cent of the total number of eucalyptus species in Australia. It was in the Blue Mountains that Darwin encountered a group of Australian aborigines still living in the wild. Speculating on their future, he wrote in his diary:

> At Sunset, by my good fortune a party of a score of the Aboriginal Blacks passed, each carrying in their accustomed manner a bundle of spears and other weapons. By giving the leading man a shilling they were easily detained and threw their spears for my amusement. They were all partly clothed and several could speak a little English; their countenances were good-humoured and pleasant and they appeared far from the degraded beings as usually represented … It is very curious thus to see in the midst of civilised people, savages, although harmless, wandering about without knowing where they will sleep and gaining their livelihood by hunting in the woods … As the difficulty of procuring food increases, so must their wandering habits; and hence the population, without any apparent deaths from famine, is repressed in a manner extremely sudden compared to what happens in civilized countries.

From the settlement of Blackheath, Darwin began the descent from the sandstone plateau of the Blue Mountains by a pass that wound down from Mount Victoria to the Bathurst Plains and which he describes as being worthy of any line of road in England. He had a letter of introduction to the superintendent of the Wallerawang property, land granted to a free settler named James Walker, which carried 15,000 sheep. The superintendent, Mr. Browne, told him that the rapidly growing prosperity on Bathurst Plains was because the brown pasture, which appears to the stranger's eye so wretched, is excellent for sheep-grazing. Wheat was now growing here, and he saw how flocks of parrots and white cockatoos had become very fond of wheat grain. The Wallerawang property was assigned forty convict labourers who had just finished shearing 7000 sheep. Darwin described the farmhouse as well stocked, but there was an absence of comfort, as not even one woman resided there.

Darwin would have expected to see kangaroos roaming the plains, and it is telling that he did not see a single one. The next day, Mr. Browne took him shooting, but there were still no signs of any kangaroos. The settlers and convicts hunted them for food and Darwin thought they would soon become extinct. Despite the lack of any large kangaroos, their greyhounds pursued a small rat-kangaroo into the hollow of a tree. If Darwin were able to examine this small marsupial closely, he would have seen that it has retained some physical characteristics of the possum and provides a link between its possum ancestors and the modern kangaroo. Darwin does not describe seeing any emus on the plains and he wrote:

> A few years since, this country abounded with wild animals; now the Emu is banished to a long distance, and the Kangaroo has become scarce, to both, the English greyhound is utterly destructive; it may be long before these animals are altogether exterminated, but their doom is fixed.

Later that day, he walked along Cox's River and was lucky enough to see one of Australia's unique and most rarely sighted creatures, the duck-billed platypus. When a specimen was first brought back to England, it was considered to be an elaborate hoax - because of its flattened body covered with seal like fur, its broad flat beaver like tail, its webbed feet and a soft snout shaped like a duck's bill, and the claim that this extraordinary creature laid eggs like a reptile. Darwin wrote in his diary:

> In the dusk of the evening, I took a stroll along a chain of ponds (which in this dry country represents the course of a river) and had the good fortune to see several of the famous Platypus. They were diving and playing in the water; but very little of their bodies were visible, so that they only appeared like so many water Rats. Mr Browne shot one; certainly it is a most extraordinary animal; the mounted specimens do not convey a proper idea of the head and beak; the latter being contracted and hardened.

While resting on the banks of the Cox's River and contemplating what he has seen that day, Darwin notices the pitfall of an Australian lion-ant beetle and observes that it constructs the same pit to catch its prey as its European counterpart. Yet since its pit is only half the size he assumes it to be a different species. He now speculates on why two lion-ants seen on opposite sides of the world should be similar but different:

> Earlier in the evening I had been lying on a sunny bank and was reflecting on the strange character of the animals of this country as compared to the rest of the world. A Disbeliever in everything beyond his own reason, might exclaim "Surely two distinct Creators must have been at work; their object however has been the same and certainly in each case the end is complete".
>
> While thus thinking, I observed the conical pitfall of a Lion-Ant; a fly fell in it and immediately disappeared; then came a large but unwary Ant … his fate however was no better than that of the poor fly. Without doubt, this predatory Larva belongs to the same genus, but a different species from the Euro-

pean one. Now, what would the Disbeliever say to this? Would any two workmen ever hit on so beautiful, so simple and yet so artificial a contrivance? It cannot be thought so. The one hand has surely worked over the whole world. A Geologist, perhaps, would suggest that the periods of Creation have been distinct and remote from one another; that the Creator rested in his labour.

In the first paragraph, Darwin is thinking about how different the animals of Australia are compared to the rest of the world and he puts the case using the person who is 'A Disbeliever in everything beyond his own reason' for two distinct Creators. Then in the second paragraph he uses the example of the lion-ant to conclude that there has been only one Creator using the person he describes as 'The Geologist', who of course could be himself, to conclude that there must have been one Creator but different periods of creation, perhaps in different parts of the world and separated by periods of geological activity.

Darwin did not see any emus while in Australia, but he certainly knew they existed, and this raised another problem. The existence of similar large flightless birds such as the rhea in South America, the emu and cassowary in Australia and the ostrich in Africa was an enigma. He had personally seen the rhea of South America and the wide distribution of these large flightless birds over all the southern continents must have been of great interest to him, as these birds could not fly across the oceans, and there was no mechanism to explain their distribution other than separate creations in different parts of the world.

Charles Darwin then accomplishes a feat of considerable endurance by riding from Wallerawang to Bathurst in a single day, a 42 kilometre journey in the heat and dust of an Australian summer, and he describes riding through clouds of dust blown by a wind so hot that it felt as if it had passed over fire. In Bathurst, he stayed in the military barracks, which housed the commander, three sergeants, twenty four rank-and-file soldiers and eleven mounted police. Convicts sent from England were normally freed after serving seven years as convict labour and given a 'ticket of leave', subject to not committing any other offences. Darwin would have listened to the conversations in the military barracks and learnt something about the 'real' Australia and about the various classes of convicts or former convicts in the district, as he explains:

> A 'squatter' is a freed or 'ticket of leave' man, who builds a hut of bark in unoccupied ground, buys or steals a few animals, sells spirits without a licence, buys and sells some stolen goods, and so at last becomes rich and turns farmer: He is the horror of all his honest neighbours. – A 'Crawler' is an assigned Convict, who runs away and lives how he can by labour and petty theft, - The 'Bush Ranger' is an open villain, who lives by highway robbery and plunder; generally they are desperate and will sooner be killed than taken alive. – In the country it is necessary, to understand these three names, for they are in perpetual use.

On his return to Sydney, Darwin visits Captain Phillip Parker King, the Australian-born commander of the *Beagle's* first surveying voyage, at his property near Penrith and then travels to Parramatta to visit King's brother-in-law Hannibal MacArthur. Here, the dinner conversations would have been about sheep, wool, acquiring wealth, as well as the never-ending debate and complaint about the new society that was being formed by the convict 'emancipists' now living together with the 'free settlers'. Darwin saw that the whole community was rancorously divided over almost every subject. How disgusting, exclaimed Darwin, to be waited on by a man who, the day before, was by your representation flogged for some trifling misdemeanour. However, later in his 1839 Journal, Darwin wrote that as a means of converting vagabonds most useless in one hemisphere into outwardly honest citizens in another, the transportation of convicts to Australia had succeeded to a degree perhaps unparalleled in history.

After the *Beagle* finished its chronometric measurements in Sydney, the next port of call was Hobart in Tasmania. Here Darwin explored the town and its surroundings, described the geology and was entertained by the Surveyor-General, George Frankland at his house at Battery Point, where Darwin said he spent 'the most agreeable evening since leaving England'. Here Darwin learnt of the disgraceful treatment of the Tasmanian aborigines by English settlers, as after just thirty years, the entire population of Tasmanian aborigines had either been murdered or banished from their native lands and sent into exile. This gave Darwin pause to think about the rapid destruction that one 'variety' of species can inflict upon another, as he wrote in his 1839 Journal:

> All the aborigines have been removed to an island in Bass's Straits, so that Van Diemen's Land enjoys the great advantage of being free from a native population. This most cruel step seems to have been quite unavoidable, as the only means of stopping a fearful succession of robberies, burnings, and murders committed by the blacks; but which sooner or later must have ended in their utter destruction. I fear there is no doubt that this train of evil and its consequences, originated in the infamous conduct of some of our countrymen. Thirty years is a short period, in which to have banished the last aboriginal from his native island, and that island nearly as large as Ireland. I do not have a more striking instance of the comparative rate of increase of a civilised over a savage people ... They were removed to Gun Carriage Island, where food and clothes were provided them. I fear from what I heard at Hobart Town that they are very far from being contented: some even think the race will soon become extinct.

This thought was correct as by 1840 the last surviving Tasmanian aborigines living in exile numbered only 100, and Darwin's sad prediction came to pass almost forty years later when the 'official history' tells us that the last remaining full-blooded member of the Tasmanian aborigines, a woman called Truganini, died at Oyster Cove outside Hobart.

Darwin felt he had achieved very little in Australia because he was no longer able to spend enough time ashore to make 'connected and therefore interesting' observations. He was anxious to get back to England, not only to reunite with his family after such a long absence, but also to commence work on the study of all the natural history collections he had sent home, and the journal and books that he intended to write. From Hobart, he wrote a letter to his cousin William Fox complaining that ever since the *Beagle* completed its surveys of South America, its only remaining task has been to complete its chain of longitude determinations around the world:

> Now that the object of our voyage is reduced simply to Chronometrical Measurements a large portion of time is spent making passages. – This is to me so much existence obliterated from the page of life, - I hate every wave of the ocean with a fervour, which you, who have only seen the green waters of the shore, can never understand.

From Hobart, the *Beagle* sailed to the settlement at King Georges Sound in Western Australia, now Albany, to take their final chronological measurement in Australia and then towards home. Darwin is more than happy to say goodbye to Australia as he wrote:

> Farewell Australia, you are a rising infant and doubtless some day will reign a great princess in the South. But you are too great and ambitious for affection, yet not great enough for respect; I leave your shores without sorrow or regret.

On the journey home Darwin writes of the several sources of enjoyment in a long voyage. The map of the world ceases to be a blank and becomes a picture full of the most varied and animated figures. Continents and islands come to life, and having sailed for weeks along portions of their shores they start to assume their proper dimensions. After some time in Cape Town, making more chronological observations, the *Beagle* rounds the Cape of Good Hope and is now in the Atlantic Ocean and heading home. Darwin contemplates life on his return to England and the fact that for the next few years he will be fully occupied classifying and documenting the huge number of specimens he has collected during his voyage around the world:

> I look forward with a comical mixture of dread and satisfaction to the amount of work, which remains for me in England. I suppose my chief residence will at first be Cambridge and then London. The latter, I fear, will in every respect turn out most convenient. I grieve to think of it; for a good walk in the true country is the greatest delight, which I can imagine.

The last months of the journey home were hard on all the crew and Darwin wrote how 'There never was a ship so full of home-sick heroes'. They had been away for almost five years and Darwin could not wait to join his family and see England's green and pleasant land. He wrote of his joy to be heading home as well as concern for the emotional state of his captain:

> I think we shall not reach England before September: But thank God the captain is as home sick as I am, and I trust that he will grow worse than better ... I have been for the last twelve months on very cordial terms with him. He is an extraordinary but noble character, unfortunately, however, affected with

strong peculiarities of temper. Of this no man is more aware than himself, as he shows by his attempts to conquer them.

I often doubt what will be his end; under many circumstances, I am sure it will be a brilliant one, under others, I fear a very unhappy one.

The *Beagle* arrived at Falmouth in Cornwall in 1836, where Charles Darwin took his leave and rushed to the family home in Shrewsbury. The *Beagle* sailed on to Plymouth, Portsmouth and Deal to receive Admiralty officials and then finally to Greenwich on the Thames to make the last in its record breaking series of chronometer readings around the globe. FitzRoy's insistence on taking so many chronometers paid off because after 5 years only half were working properly. The shift in local noon time at the Greenwich Meridian as measured by the *Beagle's* chronometers should be exactly twenty-four hours. The best of the chronometers exceeded this measurement by just 33 seconds, which is equivalent to 8.25 nautical miles (15.28 km). An impressive result for a journey of tens of thousands of miles around the world and taking over five years to complete.

Darwin returned to England as a committed Christian and still believing in the God of Nature for when recalling the highlights of his voyage on the *Beagle* he writes:

> Among the many scenes which are deeply impressed on my mind, none exceed in sublimity the primeval forests not yet defaced by the hand of man; whether those of Brazil, where the powers of life are predominant, or those of Tierra del Fuego, where death and decay prevail. Both are temples filled with the varied productions of the God of Nature – no one can stand in these solitudes unmoved, and not feel that there is more in man than the mere breath of his body.

8

Charles Darwin - In London

Charles Darwin reached Shrewsbury in the late evening, not wishing to disturb the household, he spent the night at a local inn and to their mutual delight, he walked in on his family at breakfast. Writing to Robert FitzRoy, his benefactor and companion of the last five years, he describes his joy at being home:

> My Dear FitzRoy,
> I arrived here yesterday at breakfast-time, and, thank God, found all my dear sisters and father quite well. My father appears more cheerful and very little older than when I left. My sisters assure me that I do not look the least different, and I am able to return the compliment ... I hope you will not forget to send me a note telling me how you go on ... If you do not receive much satisfaction for all the mental and bodily energy you have expended in His Majesty's service, you will be most hardly treated.
> Chas. Darwin

After three weeks of delightful reunion with his family, Darwin travelled to Greenwich to oversee the unloading of his precious collection. No naturalist since Joseph Banks had the opportunity to see so much of the world and to be able to compare the natural history of different continents as Charles Darwin. He had returned to England with thousands of specimens, enough to fill a complete museum of its own, and they would take years to study. He was not an expert on anything and needed to find those taxonomists who could describe and classify each one of them. Fortunately, Darwin was able to call on his Cambridge connections to find those experts who could help. Richard Owen took the fossil mammals, John Gould took on the birds, John Stevens Henslow looked at the plants and Thomas Bell would study the reptiles. After Joseph Hooker returned to England from his voyage to the southern continents and Antarctica, Darwin invited him to classify the plants that he had collected in South America and the Galapagos Islands. Hooker agreed and the pair began a lifelong friendship.

John Gould was particularly excited by the rather nondescript little birds from the Galapagos. Darwin had assumed they were from several different groups: wrens, finches, blackbirds etc. However, Gould believed that despite their totally different beaks they were all finches. The problem was that Darwin's collecting on Galapagos had been uncharacteristically clumsy. He had failed to completely label from which island his birds had been collected, never imagining that different islands, not far apart, would produce different birds. Gould needed to examine more Galapagos birds that were correctly labelled, and Darwin had to go to Robert FitzRoy and his own assistant, Syms Covington, to borrow their specimens.

John Gould now classified all the birds as finches and observed how their beaks had adapted to eat insects, cactus, or seeds. In the absence of other bird species, the finches had adapted to different food niches. On one island, the beaks were stronger to crack nuts and seeds, on another island, the beaks were smaller to catch insects, and on another island, the beak was especially useful for feeding on fruits and flowers. With these new specimens, Gould's initial conclusion was confirmed: here was a group of birds that were closely related, yet their beaks had adapted according to the food they ate - different islands, different finches, different species. Thomas Bell from the Royal Zoological Society, who had been identifying Darwin's reptile collection, came up with a similar conclusion, as each of the Galapagos Islands had produced its own distinct species of iguana lizard.

1. Geospiza magnirostris.
2. Geospiza fortis.
3. Geospiza parvula.
4. Certhidea olivacea.

Four species of Galapagos finch with different beaks, from *Darwin's Journal of Researches*

Darwin now realised that the Galapagos Islands represented a remarkable 'natural experiment', the ancestral finches which had arrived from the South American mainland had filled every small-bird niche on the islands and in the process acquired a whole range of unfinch-like beaks. As he wrote:

> By far the most remarkable feature in the natural history of this archipelago is that the different islands to a considerable extent are inhabited by a different set of beings. My attention was first called to this fact by the Vice-Governor Mr Lawson, declaring that the tortoises differed from the different islands, and that he could with certainty tell from which island any one was brought. I did not for some time pay sufficient attention to this statement, and I had already partially mingled together the collections from two of the islands, about 50 or 60 miles apart, and most of them in sight of each other, formed of precisely the same rocks, placed under a quite similar climate, rising to nearly equal height.

Within months of his return, Darwin achieved his ambition of joining the elite world of British science as he was elected to the Royal Society, the Geological Society, the Zoological Society and the Royal Geographic Society. At the Geological Society, he delivered three short papers describing some of his geological observations during his voyage. It was there that he met Charles Lyell for the first time. They discussed his *Principles of Geology*, and despite the age difference, they began a lifelong friendship. Darwin wrote, 'I saw more of Lyell than any other man both before and after my marriage ... he was very kind-hearted and thoroughly liberal in his religious beliefs or disbeliefs; but was a strong theist'. Lyell also gave Darwin some professional advice in this letter:

> Don't accept any official scientific place if you can avoid it, and tell no one I gave you this advice ... I fought against the calamity of being President (of the Geological Society) as long as I could ... Work as I did, exclusively for yourself and for Science for many years, and do not prematurely incur the honour or the penalty of official dignities. There are people who may

be profitably employed in such duties, because they would not work if not so engaged.

Darwin had absorbed Lyell's *Principles of Geology* and had used his geological ideas to explain the landforms and rock outcrops he saw on his voyage around the world, especially in his writings on *The Geology of South America*. He adopted Lyell's creed of gradual change and began to believe that gradual change was also important in the biological sciences. For the rest of his life, he believed in the power of small and gradual changes and saw it as one of the most important conceptual steps in his journey towards an understanding of the origin of species. Darwin wrote in a private letter:

> I always felt as if my books came half out of Lyell's brain, and that I never acknowledged this sufficiently ... the great merit of the *Principles* was that it altered the whole tone of one's mind, and therefore that, when seeing a thing never seen by Lyell, one yet saw it partially through his eyes.

Darwin obtained a Treasury grant of 1000 pounds to edit the descriptions by the experts of his collections and published them in five volumes titled *The Zoology of the Voyage of H.M.S. Beagle,* complete with lavishly illustrated hand-coloured plates. The volumes include an account of the fossil mammals by Professor Owen, the living mammals by Waterhouse, the birds by John Gould, the fish by the Rev. L. Jenyns, and the reptiles by Thomas Bell. Before leaving the *Beagle*, Darwin had agreed to contribute a third volume to FitzRoy's narrative of the voyages of the *Adventure* and the *Beagle* from 1826-1830 and then the *Beagle* from 1831– 1836. Writing to his cousin, he said:

> In your last letter you urge me, to get ready the book. I am now hard at work and give up everything else for it. Our plan is as follows. – Capt. FitzRoy writes two volumes, out of the

materials collected during both the last voyage under Captain King to Tierra del Fuego and during the circumnavigation. – I am to have the third volume, in which I intend giving a kind of journal of a naturalist, not following however, always the order of time, but rather the order of position. – The habits of animals will occupy a large portion, sketches of the geology, the appearance of the country, and personal details will make the hodge-podge complete.

Darwin spent the next two years writing and revising the narrative account of his five years on the *Beagle*. FitzRoy took even longer to complete his first two volumes, but their work was finally completed and both were published in 1939 as a three-volume set entitled *Narrative of the Surveying Voyages of HMS Adventure and Beagle between the Years 1826 and 1836 describing their examination of the southern shores of South America and Beagle's circumnavigation of the Globe*. Darwin's third volume was inauspiciously titled *Journal and Remarks, 1832 -1836*. Darwin was able to fuse both scientific writing with poetic description, and when the reviews appeared, Darwin's volume was praised and FitzRoy's volumes were ignored. The three volumes could be purchased separately and Darwin's soon became a best seller, requiring both a reprint and a grander title - *Journal of Researches into the Geology and Natural History of the various countries visited by the HMS Beagle under the command of Captain FitzRoy from 1832 to 1836*. Darwin was praised in reviews of the book and described as a 'First-rate landscape-painter with a pen'. Retitled again in the 1845 edition, his volume became *The Voyage of the Beagle* and remains one of the great travel books of the age.

Unfortunately for FitzRoy, and to his great chagrin, he became known as the captain who sailed Darwin around the world in the *Beagle*. In 1843, he was nominated as Lieutenant Governor of New Zealand, where he served for three years. Here, he faced intractable problems of Maori land rights and land-hungry white settlers, which led to a settlers' revolt, his effigy being burned, and his recall to London. For two years from 1849, he served as Superintendent of Woolwich Dockyard and oversaw the trials of the Navy's first screw-driven steamship, although he remained an unconverted sailing ship man. He resigned from the Navy in 1850 and in 1851 was elected to the Royal Society, where he developed his interest in meteorology. He was instrumental in providing port towns and the captains of all ships, both naval and maritime, with the instruments needed to measure atmospheric pressure, temperature, wind direction and humidity. This data could be used to build synoptic charts and provide weather forecasts for shipping. His work saved the loss of many lives at sea and he was promoted to Admiral in 1857 and Vice Admiral in 1863. Robert FitzRoy became known as the father of meteorology in Great Britain, yet despite his success, there was always public criticism when inevitably some weather forecasts proved to be tragically wrong.

But there was something missing in Darwin's life. He would soon be thirty years old, and his thoughts turned to marriage. He assumed that marriage must mean an end to his comfortable and carefree life as a gentleman naturalist. Like a true scientist Darwin drew up a list with two columns under the headings, Marry and Not Marry. He probably spent many hours listing the advantages and disadvantages of married life, finally writing this conclusion at the bottom of his list:

> My God, it is intolerable to think of spending one's whole life, like a neuter bee, working, working, and nothing after all. No, no won't do. Imagine living all one's day solitary in a smoky dirty London House.

He did not have to look far for the 'nice soft wife' on his list, and in November 1838, he married his cousin Emma Wedgwood, who had been his friend and companion since childhood. By marrying 'within the family', they strengthened the ties of position and money, binding the Darwin and Wedgwood dynasties, and their financial future was such that Charles Darwin could devote all his future efforts to science. The only possible problem between the happy couple was religion. Emma was firm in the religion of her upbringing, whereas Charles, even when studying to be a cleric, had never been as interested in religion. In his usual honesty, Darwin had to confess his misgivings to Emma and she responded in writing:

> I thank you from the bottom of my heart for your openness with me and I should dread the feeling that you were concealing your opinion from fear of giving me pain ... my own dear Charley we now do belong to each other and I cannot help being open with you. Will you do me a favour? ... It is to read our Saviour's farewell discourse to his disciples which begins at the end of the 13th Chap. Of John. It is so full of love to them & devotion & every beautiful feeling. It is the part of the New Testament I love best.

Charles and Emma were married at the Wedgwood family home of Maer Hall in Staffordshire, and soon after moved into a house on Gower Street in London, and the portrait of Darwin was made not long after their marriage.

About this time, his third volume of *The Narrative* was ready to be published together with that of Robert FitzRoy. Significantly, FitzRoy would have read Darwin's volume before publication and decided to add an extra chapter to his work entitled 'A Few Remarks with Reference to the Deluge', which, counter to the writings of Darwin, described the shells and fossils he had found on the plains of Argentina as evidence of the Biblical Flood. *The Voyage of the Beagle* became one of the most popular books of the period and Darwin was delighted, writing 'the success of this my first literary child, always tickles my vanity more than any of my other books'. Darwin sent a copy with a covering letter to the great Alexander von Humboldt, who was Darwin's inspiration to visit South America. Humboldt wrote in return declaring it an admirable book and saying that Darwin had an excellent future ahead of him:

> You told me in your kind letter that, when you were young, the manner in which I studied and depicted nature in the torrid zones contributed toward exciting in you the ardour and desire to travel in distant lands. Considering the importance of your work, Sir, this may be the greatest success that my humble work could bring.

During the years since the return of the *Beagle*, Darwin had always been thinking about the meaning of the Galapagos finches. They were not, as Darwin had initially thought just variations of the familiar birds found on the mainland, but as identified by the ornithologist John Gould, were different species. Why should these islands share a group of related species unknown anywhere else in the world? And why should each individual island have its own unique species?

Portrait of Charles Darwin, George Richmond, 1840

The implications were revolutionary. Since species were thought to be fixed, did this mean that God was continuously creating new ones? He had probably come to some conclusions because in the second edition of *The Voyage of the Beagle* he rewrote part of this chapter adding some carefully crafted, yet still ambiguous words:

Seeing this gradation and diversity of structure in one small, intimately related group of birds, one might really fancy that from the original paucity in the archipelago, one species has been taken and modified for different ends.

Darwin was not yet ready to make any definitive conclusions on that mystery of mysteries – the first appearance of new beings on this earth, but perhaps there was someone else who would.

9

Alfred Russel Wallace – The Early Years

Alfred Russel Wallace was born in 1823 into an impoverished middle-class family with seven children. His father, although trained as a solicitor, had never actually practised and slowly squandered his small inheritance on hopeless business ventures. The young Wallace bonded with the natural world, and he recalls his earliest childhood memories from the village of Usk in Wales:

> The form and colour of the house, the road, the river close below it, the bridge with the cottage near its foot, the narrow fields between us and the bridge, the steep wooded bank at the back, the stone quarry and the very shape and position of the flat slabs on which we stood fishing, the cottages a little further on the road ... all come before me as I recall these earlier days with a distinctness strangely contrasted with the vague shadowy figures of the human beings who were my constant associates in all these scenes.

The family regularly had to move to find cheaper accommodation and when he was about six, they moved to Hertford where he started primary school. His school had been founded in 1617, and as Wallace describes in his biography, nothing much seemed to have changed since that time:

> It consisted of one large room. There was a master's desk at each end, and two on other sides, and two open fireplaces ... As we went to school even in winter at seven in the morning, and on three days a week remained till five in the afternoon, some artificial lighting was necessary, and this was effected by the primitive method of every boy bringing his own candles or candle-ends.

Fortunately, Wallace's father had found a job in the Hertford town library and a regular stream of books passed through the household, which his father would read aloud to the children. Alfred spent every wet Saturday afternoon in the library, squatting in a corner and reading voraciously. His religious upbringing was conventional Church of England, twice to church on Sundays, and readings from the Bible at home. This was the period in his life when he felt something of a religious fervour, but he later wrote that 'as there was no sufficient basis of intelligible fact or connected reasoning to satisfy my intellect, the feeling soon left me, and has never returned'.

By the time Wallace reached twelve, his father could no longer afford to pay his school fees. Many children of his class and age left school at this time to become trade apprentices. His eldest brother was an apprentice surveyor and another brother was an apprentice carpenter. Since Alfred was clever for his age, his father arranged with the headmaster that in lieu of fees, he could stay at school and help in teaching the younger children. Wallace describes his shy, sensitive and self-conscious young self during this difficult time:

> While continuing my regular classes in Latin and Algebra, I took the younger boys in reading and dictation, arithmetic

and writing. Although I had no objection whatever to the work itself, the anomalous position it gave me in the school ... subjected me to painful insinuations and annoying remarks. I was especially sensitive to what all boys dislike – being placed in any exceptional position, or having to do anything different from other boys. Every time I entered the school room I felt ashamed.

Photo of Alfred Russel Wallace

Unlike Charles Darwin, who was born into a wealthy family and had the advantage of an education at Cambridge, Alfred Russel Wallace left school at the age of fourteen, about the same time as Darwin returned to England after the voyage of the *Beagle*. Later that same year Alfred began working as an assistant for his elder brother William in surveying a country parish in Bedfordshire. The young Alfred loved being out of the schoolroom and outside in the country. The surveying work included mapping and calculating areas using trigonometry and he was happy to find a practical application to the mathematics he had learned at school:

> I carried a flag or measuring-rod and stuck in pegs or cut triangular holes in the grass where required to form marks for future reference. We carried bill-hooks for cutting rods and pegs, as well as for clearing away branches that obstructed the view ... We started work after an early breakfast, and usually took with

us a good supply of bread-and-cheese and a half gallon of beer, and about one o'clock sat down under the shelter of a hedge to enjoy our lunch.

Wallace delighted in the countryside, going for long walks in his spare time, but knew nothing about insects, birds, flowers and trees because none of this was taught in school. Surprised there was such a subject as Botany, he used what little money he had to buy a book called *The Elements of Botany* to help identify the plants he saw on his rambles. He then experienced the joy that every new discovery gives to a lover of nature:

> I found in my walks that I lost much time in gathering the same species several times. I therefore began to form a herbarium, collecting good specimens and drying them carefully ... My brother, however, did not approve of my devotion to this study, even though I had absolutely nothing else to do ... Neither he nor I could foresee that it would have any effect on my future life.

Throughout Britain, the Mechanics' Institutes were being founded for young men like Wallace to educate themselves in practical skills. Following his interests, Wallace learned that the Swedish naturalist Carl Linnaeus had developed the discipline of taxonomy by organising flora and fauna into classes, orders, genera and species. Wallace then borrowed an Encyclopaedia of British plants and spent months copying the genera and species of all the native flora into his own copy of *Elements of Botany* and thus becoming an impressive amateur botanist.

Wallace believed that it was through education and specifically science that the human race could develop. Inspired by his own efforts at self-education, he wrote, at the age of eighteen, a five-page article 'On the Best Method of Conducting the Kington Mechanics' Institute'. With the rapid industrialisation of Britain, local businessmen saw that it was in their interest to fund the Mechanics' Institutes, because they helped provide the educated workers they needed. This and the local Lending Library provided a means of self-education for intelligent young men like Alfred Russel Wallace, eager to soak up knowledge about the world around them.

A downturn in surveying jobs meant that William had to ask his brother to look for other work. Alfred thought that teaching might be a possibility and he found a position at the Collegiate School in Leicester. The headmaster, Mr Hill, engaged him as an assistant master to teach English, Geometry, and Drawing, as well as to live in the school house and oversee the evening preparation of about twenty boarders. Wallace, now twenty years old, probably had his own room for the first time in his life and, from his own description seemed very comfortable:

> There were two assistant masters, both pleasant men. In drawing I had only beginners; but I soon found I had to improve myself, so I sketched a great deal … I had a very comfortable bedroom, where a fire was lit every afternoon in winter, so that, with the exception of one hour with the boys and half an hour at supper with Mr. and Mrs. Hill, my time after four or five in the afternoon was my own.

Leicester also had a Mechanics' Institute and Lending Library where Wallace could find books on his favourite subjects - botany, butterflies and insects. It was in 1844 and probably on one of his ramblings that Wallace met Henry Walter Bates, a young man his own age who shared a common interest in the natural world around their hometown. Bates had been forced to leave school at twelve to work as an apprentice to the hosiery trade, but his passion was for beetles. He proudly showed Wallace his large, neatly arranged collection and a thick book with the descriptions of more than 3,000 British species of beetle. Unknown to almost everybody except Henry Walter Bates, there existed around Leicester thousands of different species of beetle, of all shapes, colours and sizes. This took Wallace completely by surprise as he wrote:

> If I had been asked before how many different kinds of beetle were to be found in any small district near a town, I should probably have guessed fifty, or at the outside a hundred ... Now I learnt that ... there were probably a thousand ... within ten miles.

Wallace obtained a collecting bottle, pins, a store-box and in order to learn their names and classification, he managed to purchase 'at a wholesale price' a copy of James Stephen's *Manual of British Coleoptera*. Both young men were fortunate to have found each other at this stage in their lives. They shared their free time roaming the countryside around Leicester hunting beetles and discussing books they were reading on natural history. They both read Charles Darwin's *Journal of Research* from the voyage of the Beagle. Wallace was impressed by Darwin's accessible language and he wrote to Bates saying:

> His style of writing I very much admire, so free from all labour, affectation, or egotism, and yet so full of interest and original thought.

They both read Alexander Von Humboldt's multi-volume *Personal Narrative of Travels to the Equinoctial Regions of the New Continent* and discussed his travels in South America and the glories of the tropical rainforest. Humboldt saw that in the natural world, no single fact can be considered in isolation. He invented the web of life and the concept of nature as we know it today, including the concept of human-induced climate change. After the publication of his works, Humboldt travelled to England, where he met Sir Joseph Banks, now President of the Royal Society, who showed him his huge herbarium with its unique Australian specimens. Alexander Von Humboldt, Sir Joseph Banks and Charles Darwin were heroes to the young Wallace and Bates, yet their heroes' lives of travel, adventure and observation of natural history were something they could only dream of.

It was in February 1846, while Wallace was teaching at Leicester, that he received news of his brother William's sudden death. William had continued his surveying work in Wales and had been called to London to give evidence before a committee on the proposed South Wales Railway Bill. Returning to Wales in the cheapest transportation available, which was an open railway carriage, he caught a severe chill which was followed by sleeping in a damp bed in Bristol and brought on congestion of the lungs.

While attending his brother's funeral and speaking with his friends, Wallace learnt of the current railway boom with speculators throwing money at new railway lines to be built across Britain. Wallace had inherited his brother's surveying equipment and there was now a huge demand for surveyors. He contracted with a civil engineer who employed him to survey a line that would run up the valley from Neath to Merthyr Tydfil. Wallace received what for him was the outstanding sum of two guineas a day plus all the expenses of chain and staff men, food, hotel accommodation etc. This outdoor work took all summer and Alfred Wallace loved being out in the open air again and enjoying the natural beauty of South Wales:

> The work took me along pleasant lanes, through woods and by streams, and up one of the wildest and most picturesque glens I have ever explored. Here we had to climb over huge rocks as big as houses, ascend cascades, and take cross-levels up steep banks and precipices all densely wooded.

In 1844, a book, published anonymously and entitled *Vestiges of the Natural History of Creation,* caused a stir in drawing rooms across Britain. The book was a mixture of fact and fiction that proposed the general idea of biological evolution, supported by some provocative facts and arguments, but without any theory of how evolution might work. A huge success among less critical readers, it was dismissed by the scientific community as sensationalist junk and voraciously condemned by the Church and the Establishment. However, the book helped Wallace focus on the crucial question which had already been in his mind - if species arise by natural transformation as *Vestiges* argued, then what was the mechanism by which it occurred? Bates wrote to Wallace giving his opinion of the book and he replied from his surveying work in Wales:

> I have a more favourable opinion of the *Vestiges* than you appear to have. I do not consider it a hasty generalisation, but rather an ingenious hypothesis strongly supported by some striking facts and analogies, but which remains to be proved by more facts and the additional light which more research may throw upon the problem. It furnishes a subject for every observer of nature to attend to; every fact he observes will make either for or against it, and it thus serves both as an incitement to the collection of facts, and an object to which they can be applied when collected.

In 1847, the railway boom collapsed. Millions of pounds of shareholders' money were lost, and Wallace was out of a job, but through hard work and his natural frugality, he had managed to save the princely sum of 100 pounds. Here was a chance for these two young men to fulfil their youthful dreams and Henry Walter Bates describes the fateful letter he received from Alfred Russel Wallace:

> In late 1847 Mr A.R.Wallace ... proposed to me a joint expedition to the River Amazon, for the purpose of exploring the Natural History of its banks; the plan being to make ourselves a collection of objects, dispose of the duplicates in London to

pay for the expenses, and gather facts, as Mr Wallace expressed in one of his letters towards solving the problem of the origin of species.

Full of enthusiasm and ready for adventure, Wallace and Bates decided to pool their resources and organise an expedition to the Amazon Basin. They would finance the expedition by collecting fauna and flora for the commercial market, selling their specimens to the affluent private collectors who bought and displayed natural history specimens, as others displayed works of Art. They met in London early in 1848 to study South American plants and animals in the principle collections - butterflies at the Natural History Museum, insects at the India Museum, plants at the Kew Botanical Gardens. It was at the Natural History Museum that the young Wallace recalls meeting Charles Darwin in the hallways, although it seems that Darwin had no similar recollection. After a visit to the British Museum, Wallace wrote to Bates that he wanted to study one genus or family of insects in depth:

> I begin to feel rather dissatisfied with a mere local collection, little is learned by it. I should like to take some one family to study thoroughly, principally with a view to the theory of the origin of species. By that means I am strongly of the opinion that some definite results might be arrived at.

More importantly, they learned from the Museum curators how to preserve fragile specimens and send them back to England intact. Also, they needed to find someone who could receive and sell their specimens and be trusted to forward funds to some obscure settlement on the banks of the Amazon. Fortunately, they found Samuel Stevens who was himself a collector of British butterflies and beetles. Stevens proved an exemplary agent, selling their duplicate specimens 'to the best advantage' and insuring their consignments as soon as they could advise of despatch. He purchased the equipment they needed, found means of getting cash or credit to them in the most obscure places, advanced them funds against specimens not yet received, kept them up to date on what collectors were looking for and matters of general scientific interest. He was honest, trustworthy, efficient, and anticipated their needs and for this Wallace and Bates were eternally grateful.

Their decision to travel to the Amazon was settled when they both read a recently published book by W.H.Edwards entitled *A Voyage up the Amazon*. Edwards wrote enthusiastically about the beauty of the Amazon, including the full range of travellers' tales of Amazonian women, cannibal Indians, dangerous anacondas and flesh-eating piranhas. These stories did not seem to deter Wallace and Bates, who must have focused on his glorious descriptions of the Amazon River Basin - 'Where the mightiest of rivers rolls majestically through primeval forests of boundless extent, concealing, yet bringing forth the most beautiful and varied forms of animal and vegetable existence'.

10

Alfred Russel Wallace – The Voyages on the Amazon

In April 1848, the twenty-five year old Alfred Russel Wallace and the twenty-three year old Henry Walter Bates embarked from Liverpool, ready to fulfil their dream of collecting natural history specimens on the Amazon, mainly beetles, butterflies and birds to be sent to museums and collectors in Britain. They had arranged a low-cost sea passage on the small trading barque Mischief, on which they were the only passengers. After a twenty-nine day voyage they reached their destination, the town of Belém do Pará, at the mouth of the Amazon River and their adventure could begin. Wallace found the town did not meet the picturesque descriptions provided by William Edwards in his book *A Voyage up the Amazon*. The public buildings badly needed repair, some were completely in ruins, and he complains of the images created by 'picture-drawing travellers' that only describe 'the beautiful, the picturesque, and the magnificent'. However, in his descriptions, Bates certainly found the women of the town 'beautiful and picturesque':

> The impressions received during this first walk can never wholly fade from my mind... Amongst them were several hand-

some women, dressed in a slovenly manner, barefoot or shod in loose slippers; but wearing richly-decorated ear-rings, and around their necks strings of very large gold beads. They had dark, expressive eyes and remarkably rich heads of hair. It was a mere fancy, but I thought the mingled squalor, luxuriance and beauty of these women were pointedly in harmony with the rest of the scene; so striking, in the view, was the mixture of natural riches and human poverty.

Wallace and Bates found a house on the outskirts of town from where they could start collecting. When a naturalist enters a tropical forest for the first time, it is a life-changing experience, and Wallace describes this event with the same awe as his heroes Alexander von Humboldt and Charles Darwin before him:

> The sombre shade, scarcely illuminated by a single direct ray even of the tropical sun, the enormous size and height of the trees, most of which rise like huge columns a hundred feet or more without throwing out a single branch, the strange buttresses around the base of some ... It is here that the rarest birds, the most lovely insects, and the most interesting mammals and reptiles are to found.

Wallace and Bates settled into a routine of getting up before dawn to spend the early hours hunting for birds, then from mid-morning it was time for collecting butterflies and insects as they were most active just before the heat of the day. Then it was back to their residence for lunch and a siesta. In the late afternoon, they prepared their specimens, wrote up their notes and discussed their plans for the next days. Within a short time, they found many distinct kinds of butterflies and Wallace describes some of their successes:

We found very few insects, but almost all that we found were new to us. Our greatest treasure was the beautiful clear-winged butterfly with a bright violet patch on its lower wings, the *Hoetera esmeralda*, which we now saw and caught for the first time. Many other rare insects were also obtained, and the gigantic blue *Morphus* frequently passed us, but their undulating flight baffled all our efforts at capturing them.

After three months in Belém do Pará they sent their first shipment back to London. Fortunately, the specimens arrived in excellent condition as they had followed the advice received from the contacts they had made in London. Samuel Stevens placed the following advertisement in the journal *Annals and Magazine of Natural History*:

> SAMUEL STEVENS, NATURAL HISTORY AGENT, NO. 24 BLOOMSBURY STREET, BEDFORD SQUARE, begs to announce that he has recently received from South America Two beautiful Consignments of INSECTS of all orders in very fine Condition, collected in the province of Pará, containing numbers of very rare and some new species … For Sale by Private Contract.

Wallace's younger brother, Herbert, had started various apprenticeships after leaving school but had little success in finding employment. In fact, he dreamt of becoming a poet. Wallace suggested he join them in Brazil and arranged for Mr Stevens to pay his passage. After Herbert arrived in Belém do Pará in July 1849, the group travelled nine hundred kilometres up the Amazon in one of the vessels that regularly plied the great river. Day after day, they observed the jungle growing right down to the river banks, a living 'palisade' of leaves and lianas. They knew that here, deep in the rainforest, there is no better place to observe all the plants, insects, and animals that make up the magnificent web of life on earth. They could not wait until they finally reached the town of Santarém at the junction of the Amazon and the River Tapajós.

The diversity of butterflies in this new location seemed endless. They spent three productive months collecting the beautiful butterflies and strange beetles around Santarem and were delighted to find many specimens they had not seen in the collections in London. Habitat seemed to be important and Wallace noted that the varieties of insects, birds and monkeys differed from place to place for reasons that were not immediately apparent, and he kept asking himself questions. Why were certain monkeys only on one side of the Amazon? Why should winged creatures stick to a particular terrain? They were living out their dream, and after a successful morning collecting, they could cool off on the banks of the river, as according to Wallace:

> The Tapajós here is clear water with a sandy beach, and the bathing is luxurious; we bathe here in the middle of the day, when dripping with perspiration, and you can have no idea of the excessive luxury of it.

There is an awful lot of coffee in Brazil and Wallace soon became addicted to his morning coffee. He writes about how he once ran out of coffee and went down to the cottage of an old Indian who could speak a little Portuguese and begged him to get some coffee - " Por amor de Dios":

> There were some ripe berries on the trees, the sun was shining out, and he promised to set his little girl to work immediately. This was about ten in the morning. I went into the forest, and by about four returned, and found that my coffee was ready. It had been gathered, the pulp washed off, dried in the sun, husked, roasted, and pounded in a mortar; and in half an hour more I enjoyed one of the most delicious cups of coffee I have ever tasted.

After this idyllic period, the group decided to separate. Perhaps it was the arrival of Herbert that caused some friction between the two friends? Perhaps it was the differences in character that grew more significant in the wilds of the Amazon than in Leicester or London? Bates was more sociable, enjoying the company of other people, especially the ladies, and was happy to stay in one place for many months. Wallace was the loner, driven to travel further and further into the interior of the Amazon Basin in search of rarer and rarer specimens.

The Wallace brothers decided to travel another six hundred kilometres upstream to Barra (Manaos) a small settlement lying at the confluence of the Amazon and the Rio Negro. From here, Wallace found some rare specimens while collecting up the Rio Negro, but soon the wet season was upon them, and they returned to Barra. All travel ceased in the wet season as the rivers fill with huge torrents of water that 'roll like ocean waves and leap up at intervals, forty or fifty feet in the air, as if great subaqueous explosions were taking place'. It must have been miserable waiting out the four months of the wet season in Barra with violent thunderstorms, continuous heavy rains, every roof leaking water, and then the oppressive heat and humidity that followed during the intervals of sunshine. All Amazon travellers suffer from the mosquitoes, and Wallace found them a great torture, 'night after night we were kept in a state of feverish irritation, unable to close our eyes for a moment' some relief was obtained by burning dried cow dung if this was available, although then there was the stench to put up with. Herbert Wallace decided that he had enough of this sort of life and was going to return downstream to Belém do Pará as soon as the wet season finished and there was river transport. Alfred wrote that:

> After a year's experience it was now clear that my brother was not fitted to become a good natural history collector, as

he took little interest in birds or insects ... and would not have been likely to succeed.

Alfred Russel Wallace would continue his collecting up the Rio Negro and Herbert would make his return to England. When Herbert reached Belém do Pará after a three week journey down the Amazon, the once cheerful and healthy town was desolate. Yellow fever, carried by the mosquito, had struck the town with three quarters of the population suffering from the fever and many dead. No scientists had yet made the link between the tiny mosquito and its transmission of yellow fever or malaria, which was still thought to be caused by bad air or 'mal aria'. The symptoms of yellow fever are a high temperature, giddiness, headache and the parched yellow skin that gives the disease its name. After four or five days of being acutely ill, the patient is either dead or at the beginning of a long convalescence. Herbert Wallace fell ill with the fever and Walter Bates, who had himself only just recovered from the virus, nursed him for the next five days until he 'was taken with the black vomit' and died. Ironically, Herbert Wallace, that good-hearted unfortunate young man, who had wanted to be a poet, will be remembered by this verse he wrote while on the Amazon:

> For here upon the Amazon
> The dread mosquito bites –
> Inflames the blood with fever,
> And murders gentle sleep.
> Till, wary grown and peevish,
> We've half a mind to weep!
> But still although they torture,
> We know they cannot kill –
> All breathe to us in whispers
> That we are in Brazil.

Unaware of his brother's fate, Alfred Wallace set out in August 1850 to explore the upper reaches of the Rio Negro. The 'Black River' was so called because its waters are coloured by tannin derived from decaying vegetation which comes from the old and flat Guiana Shield, whereas the Amazon is a muddy white because of the huge volumes of sediment being eroded off the mountains in the Andes. The good news is that mosquito larvae cannot breed in the black acidic waters of the Rio Negro, hence mosquitoes were absent and Wallace noted 'this great luxury':

> After the muddy, monotonous, mosquito-swarming Amazon, it was with great pleasure we found ourselves in the black waters – black as ink they are, and well deserve their name; the shores are rugged and picturesque, and greatest luxury of all, mosquitoes are unknown except on the islands.

An endearing characteristic of Alfred Russel Wallace is his endless enthusiasm under the most difficult of conditions, and now he was excited to collect specimens of the rare and spectacular Umbrella Bird, found another three days journey up the Rio Negro. The Umbrella Birds have an umbrella shaped lid of black feathers, which is perhaps the most fully developed and the most beautiful crest of any bird known, and as Wallace writes:

> The Umbrella Bird is about the size of a crow, averaging about 18 inches in length. Its colour is entirely black, but varied with metallic blue tints on the outer margin of its feathers ... Were it not for its crest and neck plume it would appear to an ordinary observer nothing more than a short-legged crow.

Using smaller boats that could be hauled over the rapids, Wallace and his Indian paddlers ascended the celebrated falls of the Rio Negro, going further and further into relatively unknown territory until they reached the village of Arawak. Wallace describes the raging torrents that flowed down the river, and one particular day when they had to cross from one side of river to the other:

> Beds and ledges of rock spread across the river, while through the openings between them water rushed with terrific violence, forming dangerous whirlpools and breakers below. Here it was necessary to cross to the other side, in order to get up. We dashed into the current, were rapidly carried down, got among the boiling waves, then passed suddenly into still water under shelter of an island, we at length reached the other side, about a mile across.

Arawak was Wallace's first sight of a completely uncivilised indigenous village, full of naked children and their near-naked parents – the Baniwa. We can only guess at what the Indians thought at their first sight of this tall, skinny, strangely dressed white man, with his wire spectacles and an incomprehensible mania for collecting birds and insects. Here, Wallace's aim was to reach the remote rocky haunts of the 'gallo', or cock-of-the-rock bird. This orange and red bird shone out like a brilliant flame in the dark forest, especially when the male birds gathered to perform their courtship dances. He offered the Baniwa good money for every bird captured, and those who knew their nesting grounds led him on a long jungle journey, carrying their blowpipes and poisoned darts for the hunt. The Baniwa were semi-naked and slipped easily through the jungle, while Wallace got caught up on every branch and thorny vine. He wrote: 'I have no doubt they looked on me as a good illustration of the uselessness and bad consequence of wearing clothes upon a forest journey'. The group managed to return after nine days in the jungle with twelve cocks-of-the-rocks and Wallace describes when he first held a specimen of the brilliantly plumaged bird:

I was lost in admiration of the dazzling brilliancy of its soft downy feathers. Not a spot of blood was visible, not a feather was ruffled, and the soft, warm, flexible body set off the fresh swelling plumage, in a manner which no stuffed specimen can approach.

It is significant that during his time on the Upper Rio Negro, Wallace changes from being a struggling collector of natural history specimens, to being an explorer, an observer of the customs of the indigenous peoples and a travel writer. Perhaps it was the influence of the evocative writings of Alexander von Humboldt because as he continued upstream he finally reached the Brazilian border post at Maribatanas where Humboldt had been turned back by the Brazilian authorities after he tried to enter from Venezuela. For Wallace this was hallowed ground and he wished to follow the example of his boyhood hero:

Painting of the cock-of-the-rock, Smithsonian Library

> Not so much for my collections which I do not expect to be very profitable there, but because I am so much interested in the country and the people, that I am determined to see and know more of it and them, than any other traveller. If I do not get profit I hope at least to get some credit as an industrious and persevering traveller.

He then crossed into Venezuela and reached the village of San Carlos near the junction of the Casiquiare Canal. More than a century earlier a Jesuit priest had reported that a river connected the two great river systems of South America - the Orinoco and the Amazon.

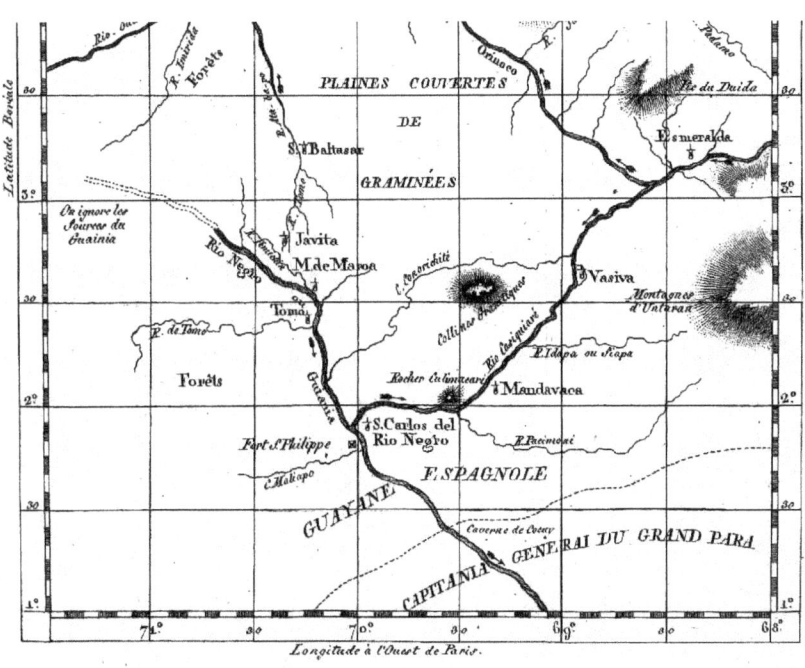

Detail from the map by Alexander von Humboldt showing the Casiquiare Canal joining the Orinoco River and the Rio Negro

All the scientists of the day said this was an impossibility, as the great river systems were always separated by a watershed or high ground. Humboldt and his companion Bonpland decided to find this mysterious Casiquiare Canal in an expedition that covered almost

3000 km of wild, mostly uninhabited jungle. They spent four months in Venezuela paddling with their Indian crews up the Rio Orinoco and then the Rio Atabapo, ascending the rapids, fighting off the mosquitos, and collecting natural history specimens as they went. Finally, in May 1800, they found the entrance to the Casiquiare Canal, and after paddling for ten days, they reached the Rio Negro and the headwaters of the Amazon at San Carlos. The Casiquiare Canal is a branch of the Upper Orinoco that meanders sluggishly south-westwards for 320 kilometres across flat forests, dropping 25 metres along the way, to join the Rio Negro and flow down into the Amazon, thus creating a rare fluvial link between two vast river systems flowing in opposite direction.

It was not until 1924 that Alexander Rice, the founder of the Harvard Institute of Geographical Exploration, completed the full journey by travelling up the Orinoco, traversing the Casiquiare Canal, and then descending down the Rio Negro and the Amazon. Alexander Rice believed in self-promotion, and an interesting feature of his work in South America was the frequent reports to the Press that he was about to be attacked by a giant anaconda or eaten by cannibals, which always seemed to be waiting around the next bend in the river. This led to this famous headline in one of the newspapers stating that 'Explorer Rice Denies He Was Eaten by Cannibals'

Wallace continued up the headwaters of the Rio Negro in a small dugout canoe until reaching Pimichin where he crossed the portage to the Rio Atabapopo and the headwaters of the Orinoco. Walking alone in the evening, he had a long wished-for encounter with one of the lords of the jungle:

> As I was walking quietly along, I saw a large jet-black animal about twenty yards before me, which took me so much by surprise that I did not at first imagine what it was. As it moved slowly on, and its whole body and long curving tail came into full view in the middle of the road, I saw that it was a fine black

jaguar ... In the middle of the road he turned his head, and for an instant paused and gazed at me, but having, I suppose, other business to attend to, walked steadily on, and disappeared into the thicket. As he advanced, I heard the scampering of small animals, and the whizzing flight of ground birds, clearing the path for their dreaded enemy.

In May 1852, after almost two years exploring the Rio Negro and the Rio Vuapés, Alfred Russel Wallace returned to Barra (Manaus) the small trading post at the junction with the Amazon River. There was a large packet of mail waiting for him and bad news from Belém do Pará:

> Mr Miller, informed me of the dangerous illness of my brother, who had been attacked by yellow fever; and when the canoe left, which brought the letter, was exhibiting such symptoms as left little hope of his recovery ... from no one could I obtain a word of information about my brother, and so remained in a state of great suspense.

Wallace was also very weak from recurring malaria, dosing himself with quinine, his delirium and fever would abate for a day or two then re-emerge in a new cycle of depression, shivering and fatigue. He could only stay close to his room, tending his menagerie of animals and wait for more news about his brother:

> Every alternate day I experienced a great depression ... this always followed a feverish night, in which I could not sleep. The next night I invariably slept well, perspiring profusely, and the succeeding day, was able to move about, and had a little appetite.

But why had there been no further news about his brother? Wallace had to find a boat and hurry down river with his mass of luggage – boxes full of specimens and his menagerie of live animals, as he had acquired twenty parrots, five monkeys, two macaws, five smaller birds, a pheasant and a toucan. The journey down the Amazon took 22 days in a small vessel loaded to the gunnels with his boxes and fitted out with a small cabin for him to sleep. On reaching Belém do Pará he tragically found his brother's cross in the town cemetery, along with the many other victims of the yellow fever outbreak. It seemed incomprehensible:

> The weather was beautiful; the summer or dry season was just commencing, vegetation was luxuriously verdant, and the bright sky and clear fresh atmosphere seemed as if they could not harbour the fatal miasma which had crowded the cemetery with funeral crosses, and made every dwelling in the city a house of mourning.

Wallace had to bring this sad news to the rest of his family and recover his own health, as he found that now any exertion brought on shivering and sickness. Ten days later, on 12 July 1852, and after all his collections were loaded, he was helped on board the brig *Helen*. Wallace was expecting to return home in triumph from his four years on the Amazon. His last consignment of duplicates had been shipped to Stevens a year earlier. With more time and in better health, he would have split up the shipment, but on board the *Helen* was his entire personal collection of ten thousand bird skins, a large herbarium of dried plants, an unparalleled collection of birds' eggs, all his numerous butterflies and insects, and his menagerie of live animals. As well as his diaries and books of sketches of his explorations of the Amazon, the Rio Negro and the Rio Vuapés.

The *Helen* was carrying a cargo of rubber, cocoa and most importantly a resinous substance used in making varnishes and lacquers. After 26 days at sea, this volatile substance caught fire, and the ship was burned to the waterline. All was lost and the only things Wallace recovered were a few personal items:

> I went down into the cabin, now suffocating hot and full of smoke, to see what was worth saving. I got my watch and a small tin box containing some shirts and a couple of old note-books, with some drawings of plants and animals, and scrambled up with them on deck.

Wallace was given a rope and told to lower himself into the lifeboat, too weak to support his own bodyweight he burned the skin off his hands as he slid down the rope and tumbled into the lifeboat. From the lifeboats the captain and crew watched in the darkness as the *Helen* went up in flames. They then drifted for ten days in the lifeboats, with them all being blistered by the sun and running out of water before they were picked up by another vessel bound for England. Wallace arrived in the port of Deal on October 1, 1852 and wrote:

> Oh glorious day! Here we are on shore at Deal, where the ship is at anchor. Such a dinner, with our two captains! Oh, beef-steaks and damson tart, a paradise for hungry sinners.

Wallace now had time to consider the magnitude of his loss. He was alive. He was back in England. But he had lost his brother and his entire personal collection, along with all his notebooks and sketch books. What might have brought him some fame or at least a comfortable life was now gone, and he wrote:

> With what pleasure had I looked upon every rare and curious insect I have added to my collection! How many times, when almost overcome by the ague (malaria) had I crawled into the forest and been rewarded by some unknown and beautiful

species! How many places where no European had set foot but my own had trodden would have been recalled to my memory by the rare birds and insects they had furnished to my collection! How many weary days and weeks had I passed, upheld only by the final hope of bringing home many new and beautiful forms from these wild regions: every one of which would be endeared to me by the recollections they would call up ... And now everything was gone, and I had not one specimen to illustrate the unknown lands I had trod, or to call back the recollections of the wild scenes I had beheld! ... Almost all the reward of my four years of privation and danger was lost. What I had hitherto sent home had little more than paid my expenses ... All my private collection of insects and birds since I left Belém had been with me. It comprised hundreds of new and beautiful species, which would have rendered my cabinet, as far as regards American species, one of the finest in Europe.

For lesser men this might have been an irrecoverable blow, but Alfred Russel Wallace would face the future with patience, equanimity, and continue to retain his endless enthusiasm under the most difficult conditions.

11

Charles Darwin - At Down House

Before Alfred Russel Wallace returned to England, Charles and Emma Darwin had settled in Gower Street in London. However, Charles was already showing signs of the illness that would plague him for the rest of his life and he could not take the strain of city living. In 1842, they moved fifteen miles out of London to Down House near Bromley in Kent, surrounded by fields and woods. This was somewhere where children could run and play, and where a naturalist could walk and think. Life in the country allowed Darwin to observe nature at close hand, to walk in the surrounding meadows and woodlands, and to undertake his studies without the interruption of a London social life.

At Down House, Darwin wrote and published three more volumes from his observations and material collected during his voyage around the world - *Structure and Distribution of Coral Reefs*, *Geological Observations on the Volcanic Islands Visited during the Voyage of the Beagle* and *Geological Observations on South America*. By October 1846, he was finally finished with all the works derived from his voyage on the *Beagle* and wrote to his mentor, John Stevens Henslow:

> You cannot think how delighted I am at having finished all my *Beagle* materials ... it is now ten years since my return, and your words, which I thought preposterous, are come true, that it would take twice the number of years to describe, than it took to collect and observe.

Darwin continued thinking about the significance of all the creatures on the Galapagos Islands. He now saw the archipelago as a little world within itself and had written that in this little world 'we seem to be brought somewhat near to that great fact – that mystery of mysteries – the first appearance of new beings on this earth'. In thinking about the Galapagos Islands, he was forced to answer some fundamental questions. Was the world created in six days and six nights as described in the Book of Genesis? Or had it evolved from something more primitive and was changing still? As the islands themselves were of recent volcanic origin, there were only two possible explanations – either God had created these species specifically for the Galapagos, or in their geographical isolation, they had evolved from a common ancestor that had migrated to the islands! Darwin was not convinced by the theory of natural transformation or transmutation proposed by the French naturalist Jean-Baptiste Lamarck. Who in 1800 wrote that individuals are influenced by their environment, and the primary mechanism of species transformation was by use-inheritance, whereby organs are developed or are diminished by use or disuse, and that the resulting changes can be transmitted to future generations. In his autobiography, Darwin wrote:

> In October 1838, that is, fifteen months after I had begun my systematic enquiry I happened to read for amusement Malthus on Population, and being well prepared to appreciate the struggle for existence which everywhere goes on from long-continued observation of the habits of animals and plants, it at once struck me that under these circumstances favourable variations

would tend to be preserved, and unfavourable ones to be destroyed. The result of this would be the formation of a new species. Here, then, I had at last got a theory by which to work, but I was so anxious to avoid prejudice that I determined for some time not to write even the briefest sketch of it. In June 1842, I first allowed myself the satisfaction of writing a very brief abstract of my theory in pencil in 35 pages; and this was enlarged during the summer of 1844 into one of 230 pages, which I had fairly copied out and still possess.

It is almost impossible today to understand the reluctance Darwin felt about sharing or publishing his idea. His theory threatened to undermine the faith in God and the Church that had become part of the social fabric and social order of Victorian England. Some will remember the hymn that children sang every week in Church Sunday School, which told us that it was not just the order of nature that was the work of the Creator, but also the structure and order of society:

> All things bright and beautiful,
> All creatures great and small,
> All things wise and wondrous,
> The Lord God made them all.
> Each little flower that opens,
> Each little bird that sings,
> He made their glowing colours,
> He made their tiny wings.
> And then it continues:
> The rich man in his castle,
> The poor man at his gate,
> GOD made them, high or lowly,
> And ordered their estate.

In January 1844, Darwin felt the need to share his big idea with somebody. He took the important step of writing to the 26-year-old botanist Joseph Hooker, who had previously sailed as the naturalist on a voyage to the southern continents and Antarctica. He was a friend and colleague whom he could trust to secrecy as he was about to confess to a murder:

> I have been now ever since my return engaged in very presumptuous work ... I was so struck with the distribution of the Galapagos organisms ... and with the character of the fossil American mammifers ... that I determined to collect blindly every sort of fact, which could bear in any way on what are species ... At last gleams of hope have come, and I am almost convinced (quite contrary to the opinion I started with) that species are not (it is like confessing a murder) immutable. Heaven forfend me from the Lamark nonsense of a 'tendency to progression', 'adaptations from the slow willing of animals' etc. But the conclusions I am led to are not widely different from his. Though the means of change are wholly so. I think I have found out (here's the presumption!) the simple way by which species become exquisitely adapted to various ends. You will now groan, and think to yourself, 'On what a man I have been wasting my time and writing to'. I should, five years ago have thought so.

Except for sharing his ideas with Joseph Hooker, Darwin decided to keep his work secret. The idea of the transmutation of species was an anathema to most respectable scientists and heresy to conservative Christian England. Darwin, his wife Emma, and all his family and friends were 'conservative Christians' and his big dangerous idea would be in his own words 'like confessing to a murder' and not just any murder. This was the murder of the belief in God as the Creator.

Darwin himself had slowly lost his faith. Emma and their children would regularly attend Sunday service at the Church, which was just a short walk from their house. Darwin would accompany the family to Church but then continue his walk or return home before the service commenced, and as he later tried to explain:

> Whilst on board the *Beagle* I was quite orthodox, and I remember being heartily laughed at by several of the officers (though themselves orthodox) for quoting the Bible as an unanswerable authority on some point ... By further reflecting that the clearest evidence would be requisite to make a sane man believe in the miracles by which Christianity is supported, - that the more we know of the fixed laws of nature the more incredible do miracles become ... I gradually came to disbelieve in Christianity as a divine revelation.
>
> I was very unwilling to give up my belief ... but I found it more and more difficult, with free scope given to my imagination, to invent evidence which would suffice to convince me. Thus disbelief crept over me at a very slow rate, but was at last complete.

His secret burned within him. This was an important contribution to scientific knowledge, something which he had dreamed of making even before embarking on the *Beagle*. What if he were to die and his idea were to die with him? In July 1844, he carefully wrote a 230 page 'Essay' of his ideas on the transmutation of species, which concluded with this beautifully crafted paragraph:

> From death, famine, rapine, and the concealed war of nature we can see that the highest good, which we can conceive, the creation of the higher animals has directly come. Doubtless it at first transcends our humble powers, to conceive laws capable of creating individual organisms, each characterised by the

most exquisite workmanship and widely-extended adaptations. It accords better with the lowness of our faculties to suppose each must require the fiat of a creator, but in the same proportion the existence of such laws should exalt our notion of the power of the omniscient Creator. There is a simple grandeur in the view of life with its powers of growth, assimilation and reproduction, being originally breathed into matter under one or a few forms, and that whilst this our planet has gone circling on according to fixed laws, and land and water, in a cycle of change, have gone on replacing each other, that from so simple an origin, through the process of gradual selection of infinitesimal changes, endless forms most beautiful and most wonderful have been evolved.

Charles Darwin then sealed his 'Essay' in an envelope and addressed it to his wife as 'Only to be opened in the Event of my Death'. Darwin could now lean back in the chair in his study and relax, as his bid for immortality lay secure in the envelope. The quiet country life loved by him and his family could continue and his reputation as a respected scientist would remain intact. The envelope also contained a long accompanying letter which began with this request:

> My Dear Emma,
> I have just finished my sketch of my species theory. If, as I believe that my theory is true and if it be accepted by even one competent judge, it will be a considerable step in science.
> I therefore write this, in case of my sudden death, as my most solemn and last request, which I am sure you will consider as if legally entered in my will, that you will devote £400 to its publication, and further will yourself, or through Hensleigh (Emma's brother), take trouble in promoting it.

Darwin had no wish to be on a collision course with the Church and its belief in a creating God. The Church of England was no longer based on an infallible church, nor an infallible bible, but upon proper reasoning and conscience. For centuries, it was the handiwork of God in nature that was the reference for the Church of England, and this explains why his big, dangerous idea would cause such a shock.

Charles Darwin's study at Down House, R Brown

Comfortable in his marriage, his science, and in his life at Down House, Darwin hardly left this rural world, except for treatment for his bouts of illness, including chronic nausea, headaches, abdominal pain, palpitations and insomnia, all of which had his doctors completely puzzled. He may have become infected with some virus or parasite during his travels through South America or as some have suggested it may have been a psychosomatic illness related to the big dangerous idea he had decided to keep secret. He was engaged in the most revolutionary of thoughts which he could not bring himself to publish or even share except with a few close friends and this may have affected his health. Darwin tried many cures which today would be considered as 'quackery', these only provided some temporary relief and he continued to be plagued by illness for the rest of his life. Darwin describes his continuing illness and how severely it affected his style of life:

> Few persons can have lived a more retired life than we have done. Besides short visits to the houses of relations, and occasionally to the seaside or elsewhere, we have gone nowhere. During the first part of our residence, we went a little into society, and received a few friends here; but my health almost always suffered from the excitement, violent shivering and vomiting attacks being thus brought on. I have therefore been compelled for many years to give up all dinner parties; and this has been somewhat of a deprivation to me, as such parties always put me into high spirits. From the same cause I have been unable to invite here very few scientific acquaintances.

In 1844, the same year that Darwin wrote his 'Essay' for posthumous publication, the publication by an anonymous author of a book called *Vestiges of the Natural History of Creation* stunned Darwin and could only have made his medical condition worse. It was written in a journalistic style, but amid all the dubious science, it proposed the evolution of all living creatures from a simple form, which was similar to his own ideas. The book sold out, a publishing sensation; it was discussed in all the fashionable clubs, around household dining tables, and in the working-class Mechanics' Institutes. What was shocking was the backlash from the scientific and religious establishment. The scientific and church communities lined up to denounce the book's errors and its insult to religion. Darwin was shaken to the core by a denunciation from his old mentor and Professor of Geology at Christ's College, the Reverend Adam Sedgwick:

> If the book be true, the labours of sober induction are in vain; religion is a lie; human law is a mass of folly, and a base injustice; morality is moonshine, our labours for the black people of Africa were works of madness; and man and women are only better than beasts.

In 1847, Darwin decided to take the important step of sending his complete 'Essay' to his confidant Joseph Dalton Hooker, who was now the botanist with the Geological Survey of Great Britain. Hooker was a medical graduate from Glasgow University who at the age of twenty received a proof copy of Darwin's forthcoming *Voyage of the Beagle* and decided he wanted to follow in his footsteps. Two years later, he sailed as the Assistant Surgeon and volunteer naturalist on the HMS *Erebus* with Captain James Clark Ross, on a voyage to the southern continents and Antarctica. As a result of their shared interests and similar experiences, Darwin and Hooker became life-long friends and collaborators. As Darwin described it they were 'co-circum-wanderers and fellow labourers'. Hooker responded with notes giving Darwin critical feedback on his 'Essay', and their correspondence continued throughout the development of Darwin's theory. If Darwin was to publish his work on the origin of species, he needed absolute scientific proof, and he thought this may lie in a detailed study of barnacles. In a letter to Joseph Hooker he tells of his plans:

> I am going to begin some papers on the lower marine animals, which will last me some months, perhaps a year, and then I shall begin looking over my ten year long accumulation of notes on species and varieties, which with writing, I dare say will take me five years.

Jean-Baptiste Lamarck, the French proponent of transmutation, believed that if all species had evolved from single-celled life forms, then marine invertebrates were the key to understanding how all higher life forms had evolved. Charles Darwin had returned from his voyage on the *Beagle* with 1,529 barnacle specimens bottled in spirits. He had been able to call on an array of experts to classify his Beagle collection of fossil mammals, birds, plants and reptiles. Yet there was no one who could classify the barnacles, as the amount of variation within these sea creatures had made them very difficult to classify. If Darwin, who was not yet an expert on anything, could classify the world's barnacles, then he would become a scientist of authority and perhaps find the scientific proof needed for his theory on the origin of species.

Comfortable in his study at Down House, his one year study of barnacles was to extend for the next ten years. His letter 'To be opened in the Event of my Death' outlining his theory of evolution remained in the drawer of his desk and the posthumous recognition of his great scientific achievement was ensured. Now in poor health, it was better to enjoy the small pleasures of his research and country life than to rock the establishment boat. His grandfather, Erasmus Darwin, had challenged the Establishment, Church and Society, but his grandson had no wish to disturb his life at Down House.

Perhaps as the result of the death of his mother when he was only eight years old, Charles Darwin needed to be loved and to please everybody. We can understand how important this was to him from a letter he wrote to his eldest son William, while his son was away at boarding school:

> You will surely find that the greatest pleasures in life is in being beloved; and this depends almost more on pleasant manners ... Depend upon it, that the only way to acquire pleasant manners is to try to please everybody you come near, your school-fellows, servants and everyone. Do, my own dear Boy, sometimes think over this, for you have plenty of sense and observation.

12

Alfred Russel Wallace - In Singapore and Borneo

Alfred Russel Wallace arrived in London in October 1852. After losing his personal collection of specimens in the sinking of the ship *Helen* and then his rescue from a lifeboat in the mid-Atlantic, his only clothing was 'a suit of the thinnest calico'. Fortunately, he was met by his agent, Samuel Stevens, who provided him with some warm clothes and some ready cash. Fortunately, Stevens had insured Wallace's returning collection for £200, a sum which helped support Wallace and his family while he tried to recover from the loss of all his Amazon collection:

> I have lost a number of sketches, drawings, notes and observations on natural history, besides the three most interesting years of my journal, the whole of which, unlike any pecuniary loss, can never be replaced; so you will see that I have some need of philosophic resignation to bear my fate with patience and equanimity ... and to occupy myself with the state of things which actually existed.

Perhaps Wallace could earn some money by writing a book? The small tin box, which he had randomly saved from the wreck, contained a set of pencil drawings of all the different species of palms in the Amazon, together with his notes as to their distribution and uses. He spent the first half of 1853 writing his book, *Palm Trees of the Amazon and their Uses,* which was published with a print run of 250 copies and sold with only limited success. He would have to make money from his next book *A Narrative of Travels on the Amazon and Rio Negro, with an Account of the Native Tribes, and Observations on the Climate, Geology, and Natural History of the Amazon Valley,* which had a print run of 750 copies, yet a decade later only 500 copies had been sold. Even today, it is a lively travel account, a wonderful read, and a remarkable achievement considering he had lost most of his notes, journals and collections. Unlike the popularity of Humboldt's and Darwin's books on travel and natural history, Wallace was not going to make a living from his writing.

The only solution was another collecting expedition. In this, he was aided by the contacts he was making in the London scientific world. Samuel Stevens introduced Wallace to the Entomological Society of London, and its members must have suffered with him, when listening to his account of the tragic loss of his specimens and his miraculous rescue from the mid-Atlantic. The President of the Society commended Wallace for risking his life in his devotion to collecting and reminded its members how they owed everything to the field collector who 'devotes his time, by night and by day; at all seasons, in all weathers; at home and abroad, to the positive capture and preservation of specimens'. The President of the Entomological Society organised a special General Meeting which created a new class of members as the revised by-laws would 'admit working entomologists to the advantage offered by the Society's meetings, Library and Collection'. This was, in fact, a major achievement because Victorian society was such that 'workers' were not normally accepted into the Societies formed by the 'gentlemen'. The President had to emphasise the value of the 'actual collector' compared to the 'experts' in the museums of London and the 'gentlemen enthusiasts' in the rectories and country houses of Britain:

> Such men do great, permanent and continual good: they tender our science an unquestionable service, and their motives are no more to be called in question than those of an artist or the author, who receives the just reward for his well-directed labours.

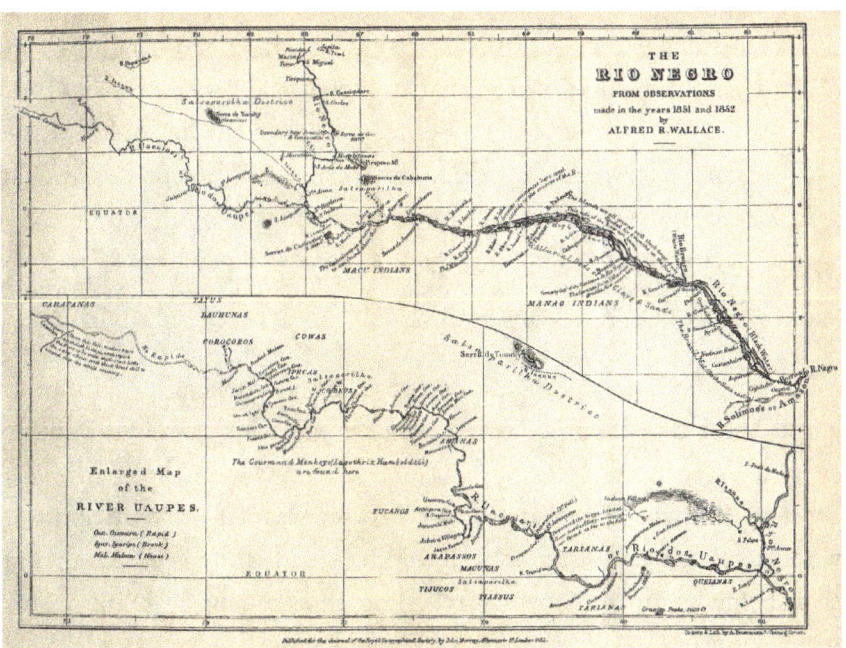

Maps of the Rio Negro and the Rio Vapes from the observations of Alfred Russel Wallace, The Royal Geographical Society

Wallace was also invited to lecture at the Royal Geographical Society, and his maps of the Rio Negro and the Rio Vaupés were published in the Journal of the Royal Geographical *Society*. His actual profession was as a surveyor, so with only a prismatic compass and a pocket sextant, he had produced remarkably accurate maps of previously uncharted rivers, while all the time battling rapids, waterfalls, recalcitrant Indian paddlers and suffering from malaria.

Wallace now became interested in Southeast Asia and he spent long hours in the Natural History Museum examining their collections, making notes and sketches of the rarer and more valuable species of birds, butterflies, and beetles found in the various islands of the Malay Archipelago:

> During my constant attendance at the meetings of the Zoological and Entomological Societies, and visits to the insect and bird departments of the British Museum, I had obtained sufficient information to satisfy me that the very finest field for an exploring and collecting naturalist was to be found in the great Malayan Archipelago, of which just sufficient was known to prove its wonderful richness, while no part of it, with the exception of the Island of Java, had been well explored as regards its natural history.

Importantly, he was able to meet Sir James Brooke, the 'White Rajah of Sarawak', when he visited London and who promised Wallace every assistance in exploring his state of Sarawak on the south-west coast of Borneo. The young James Brooke was a British adventurer who had sailed up the Sarawak River, befriended the local Rajah and then helped him put down a rebellion that had been going on for many months. In return, he was granted some land and persuaded to stay and rid the coast of pirates, which he did with the help of the British Navy. Brooke then acquired or was granted more land, defeated more uprisings and gained the respect of the Malay, Chinese and the native Dayak populations. He was knighted by the British Government in 1847 and became Sir James Brooke, the 'White Rajah of Sarawak', who now ruled over his own country.

Wallace approached the Royal Geographical Society to sponsor his voyage to Singapore and proposed to spend a year in each of six groups of islands - Borneo, the Philippines, Celebes (Sulawesi), Timor, the Moluccas (Maluku) and New Guinea, to investigate the natural history of the islands. His application was read before the Committee on Expeditions, and after some discussion, it was resolved that:

> In order to enable Mr Wallace to prosecute with success the scientific objects of his voyage, Sir Roderick Murchison be requested to apply to HM's Government to grant Mr Wallace a free passage to Singapore and to procure letters of introduction for him from the Governments of Spain and Holland to their East India Colonies.

After his application was successful, Wallace recruited a sixteen-year-old assistant, Charles Allen, and in March 1854, they sailed with first-class tickets to the Far East and the British ruled Straits Settlements. Singapore was the regional entrepot for all the trade coming from China and across the archipelago, and in its streets and around its harbour, he found the Chinese, Malays, Indians, Arabs, Javanese and Sumatrans who traded in the islands' products, as well as the English and Dutch colonialists who ruled these lands. The energetic Chinese were busy cutting down the forest in the central part of the island for timber to build the expanding colony and to clear space for plantations of pepper, nutmeg and gambir for export. He found accommodation on the outskirts of the settlement in a Jesuit mission near *Bukit Timah* (Tin Hill) and began collecting all the insects and beetles that were thriving in the piles of bark and sawdust left by the woodcutters. Wallace describes the daily routine of himself and his assistant, Charles Allen:

> Get up at half-past five, bath, and coffee. Sit down to arrange my insects of the day before, and set them in a safe

> place to dry. Charles mends our insect nets, fills our pin-cushions, and gets ready for the day. Breakfast at eight; out to the jungle at nine. We have to walk up a steep hill to reach it, and arrive dripping with perspiration. Then we wander about in the delightful shade along paths made by the Chinese woodcutters till two or three in the afternoon, generally returning with fifty or sixty beetles, some very rare or beautiful, and perhaps a few butterflies. Change clothes to sit down to kill and pin insects, Charles doing the flies, wasps and bugs; I do not trust him yet with the beetles. Dinner at four, then at work again until six. Then read or talk, or, if insects are very numerous, work again till eight or nine. Then to bed.

They collected as many as 700 species of beetles, but as many collectors had been here before him, few were rarities. It is hard for anyone visiting modern-day Singapore to comprehend that just 150 years ago, man-eating tigers roamed the jungles of this city-state. Wallace mentions that tigers killed an average of one person every day, principally those working in the plantations, and from their residence at the Jesuit mission, they would hear tigers roar once or twice in the evenings. Collecting natural history specimens was not without risk from tigers or the tiger traps, as described by Wallace:

> Here and there, too, were tiger-pits carefully covered over with sticks and leaves and so well concealed, that in several cases I had a narrow escape from falling into them. They are shaped like an iron furnace, wider at the bottom than the top and are perhaps fifteen or twenty feet deep, so that it would be almost impossible for a person unassisted to get out of one. Formerly, a sharp stake was stuck erect in the bottom, but after an unfortunate traveller had been killed by falling on one, its use was forbidden.

For exotic specimens, he would need to look further afield, and they found a vessel sailing to Malacca, one of the Straits Settlements on the Malay Peninsula. Malacca had been occupied since 1511 first by the Portuguese, then by the Dutch, and finally by the British. The inhabitants comprised the Malays, the Chinese, and the descendants of the various occupying nationalities, especially the Portuguese. As Wallace describes it, the old fort, the large Government House and the ruins of the cathedral are reminders of the former wealth and importance of this place, which was once as much the centre of Eastern trade as Singapore is now. From Malacca, they worked their way inland to Mount Ophir, where Wallace collected many beautiful butterflies and, if you can believe it, centipedes and scorpions a foot long. Sir James Brooke was now in Singapore to testify before a special commission set up to investigate his controversial anti-piracy activities. The Rajah had invited Alfred Russel Wallace to visit Sarawak when they had met in London, and now was the time to take up his invitation.

Wallace came to know Sir James well and was impressed with the relationship he had formed with the primitive Dayak people of Sarawak, who had been oppressed and enslaved under the previous Malay rulers:

> I have now seen a good deal of Sir James, and the more I see of him, the more I admire him. With the highest talents for government he combines the greatest goodness of heart and gentleness of manner ... It is a unique case in the history of the world for a European gentleman to rule over two conflicting races of semi-savages with their own consent, without any means of coercion, and depending solely on them for protection and support.

In Sarawak, virgin rainforest extended for hundreds of miles in every direction over the coast, plains and mountains. Wallace found a perfect location for collecting beetles and butterflies on the Simunjon

River. Here, Chinese and Dayak labourers were clearing the forest to develop a coal mine and were cutting a swath through the jungle for a railway line to transport the coal to the river. Everywhere there was cut timber, sawdust and bark lying on the ground, rich grounds for collecting beetles and the butterflies attracted to the sunny clearings. In one memorable day, he collected 76 different species of beetle, of which 34 were new to Wallace.

The Rajah Brooke's birdwing or Trogonoptera brookiana

The butterflies were spectacular, including this magnificent specimen:

> This beautiful creature has very long and pointed wings, almost resembling a sphinx moth in shape. It is deep velvety black, with a curved band of spots of a brilliant metallic green colour extending across the wings from tip to tip, each spot be-

ing shaped exactly like a small triangular feather, and having very much the effect of a row of the wing coverts of the Mexican trogon laid upon black velvet. The only other marks are a broad neck-collar of vivid crimson, and a few delicate white touches on the outer margins of the hind wings. This species, which was then quite new, and which I named after Sir James Brook, was very rare.

Once, while out collecting, Wallace heard a rustling in a nearby tree. He looked up and saw his first orangutan, its hair a remarkable orange colour, moving from branch to branch. He followed it through the jungle as it slowly swung from tree to tree, and found its nest formed of sticks and boughs placed in a forked branch. Since Wallace was a collector, he had no compunction in shooting and skinning at least fifteen of these 'men of the forest' (*orang hutan*, in Malay) to send back to collectors in England. He once found an orphaned baby lying in the mud where she fell after he had shot her mother for his collection. A young orangutan spends its first six months hanging on to its mother and the baby was quite comfortable hanging on to Wallace and placing her tiny hands in his large beard, and like a human baby she would cry when laid down by herself. Wallace fed her by bottle, but his hopes of introducing his little girl to London Society were dashed when she failed to thrive:

> Unfortunately, I had no milk to give it, as neither Malays, Chinese, nor Dyaks ever use that article, I in vain inquired for any female animal that could suckle my little infant. I was therefore obliged to give it rice-water from a bottle with a quill in the cork, which after a few trials it learned to suck very well. This was a very meagre diet, and the little creature did not thrive well on it, although I added sugar and cocoa-nut milk occasionally, to make it more nourishing. When I put a finger in its mouth, it sucked with great vigour, drawing in its cheeks

with all its might in the vain effort to extract some milk, and only after persevering for a long time would it give up in disgust, and set up a scream very like a baby in similar circumstances.

Returning to Kuching, Wallace was invited to spend Christmas with Rajah Brooke and his entourage at their mountain retreat. After months alone with his assistant, Wallace found their company stimulating and their conversations were wide ranging. The Rajah was a firm creationist, but he loved debate, and his Secretary later wrote that 'although Wallace could not convince us that our ugly neighbours, the orang-utans, were our ancestors, he pleased, delighted and instructed us by his clever and inexhaustible flow of talk'.

Wallace wrote three papers on the orangutan. The first is entitled *On the Orang-utan or Mias of Borneo* and the second entitled *On the Habits of the Orang-utan of Borneo*. Wallace was the first naturalist to observe and describe orangutans in their natural habitat. He also observed that the orang-utan had the same number of teeth, of the same type, and in the same position as humans. These similarities to human form and behaviour must have made an impression because in his third paper, he raised an entirely new idea, which was the possible descent of both humans and the orangutan from some common ancestor. Although his speculative view appears to have been entirely overlooked at the time, this, in 1855, may have been the first time a scientist had written of the possibility of an ape-like species taking human form:

> With what anxious expectation must we look forward to the time when the progress of civilisation in these hitherto wild countries may lay open the 'monuments of a former world', and enable us to ascertain approximately the period when the present species of Orangs first made their appearance, and perhaps prove the former existence of an allied species still more gigan-

tic in their dimensions, and more or less human in their form and structure.

During the rainy season, Wallace found himself holed up in a small house near the impressive mass of Mount Santubong, which, with its sheer limestone cliffs, marks the entrance to the broad reach of the Sarawak River, which is navigable as far inland as the settlement of Kuching and the residence of the Rajah. Wallace describes his situation there:

> I was alone with only a Malay boy as cook, and during the evenings and wet days I had nothing to do but to look over my books and ponder over the problem which was rarely absent from my thoughts ... given a mass of facts as to the distribution of animals all over the world, it occurred to me that these had never been properly utilised as indications of the way in which species had come into existence.

Wallace had embarked on his expedition up the Amazon and now across Borneo with the question of the origin of species already in his mind. With the rainy season holding up his collecting, he had time to put his facts and ideas on paper and wrote an essay ambitiously titled *On the Law Which Has Regulated the Introduction of New Species*. He finished the essay in February 1855 and shipped it off to England, where the editorial board of the *Annals and Magazine of Natural History* decided to publish what has become known as his 'Sarawak Law'. The key argument, based on his own extensive observations, was that new species and an allied genus were normally found in the same geographic area. In his essay, Wallace set out his simple law - 'That every species has come into existence coincident both in space and time with a pre-existing closely allied species'. A simple law based on his own observations in the Amazon and Borneo, he still had no explanation of how this happened but he hoped to at least start a discussion and perhaps even obtain a response from Charles Darwin based on his observations in the Galapagos Islands.

Apart from Darwin's unpublished 'Essay', this was entirely new thinking on the origin of species, and Wallace eagerly awaited a response from the scientific community in England. He did get a response from a few friends, but otherwise, there was silence. There are some factors that may explain this. Firstly, where was he? Certainly not at the meetings of the Entomological Society or the Zoological Society in London, but somewhere out in the wilds of Borneo. Secondly, he was not a 'gentleman expert'; he had no social standing or even any fixed address. Thirdly, he was not a naturalist but a 'commercial' collector who sold insects, butterflies and stuffed birds for a living - surely his opinions could not count for very much.

His friend Henry Bates was still collecting in the Amazon when he read Wallace's 'Sarawak Paper'. Bates was also at the front line of the species question, and they must have discussed it many times while together in the jungles of the Amazon. He wrote an enthusiastic response to Wallace:

> I was startled at first to see you are already ripe for the enunciation of the theory. You can imagine with what interest I read and studied it, and I must say that it is perfectly well done. The idea is like truth itself, so simple and obvious that those who read and understand it will be struck by its simplicity; yet it is perfectly original ... Few men will be in a condition to comprehend and appreciate the paper, but it will infallibly create for you a high and sound reputation.

Bates' letter must have come from the Amazon to London and perhaps to Samuel Stevens and then forwarded to Wallace who was by now somewhere in the Indonesian Archipelago. The species question was always on Wallace's mind and after the many months that it took for the letter to reach him, he responded to Bates:

> The great difficulty is to understand how, if one species was gradually changed into another, there continued to be so many quite distinct species, so many which differed from their nearest allies by slight yet perfectly definite and constant characters.

Charles Darwin did not see Wallace's 'Sarawak Paper' as either particularly interesting or pointing to the evolution of species and wrote in the margins of his copy 'nothing very new' and 'it all seems like creation to him'. However, in April 1856, Charles Lyell spent a few days at Down House and it was during this stay that Darwin revealed the theory he had been quietly developing over the last eighteen years - his theory of natural selection. Lyell, even though himself an orthodox creationist, was more observant and warned Darwin that Wallace was heading towards this same conclusion. In fact, Wallace indirectly referred to Darwin when in his 'Sarawak Paper' he wrote of the importance of the study of islands and demanded why the variation of the species found on the Galapagos had not received any sort of explanation:

> Such phenomena as are exhibited by the Galapagos Islands, which contain little groups of plants and animals peculiar to themselves, but most nearly allied to those of South America, have not hitherto received any, even a conjectural explanation.

Of course it was Charles Darwin who had famously described the Galapagos fauna and flora. Unknown to Wallace, his more than conjectural explanation, his 230 page 'Essay' on the origin of species, remained locked in his desk drawer at Down House.

Wallace had spent almost fifteen months collecting in Sarawak and he returned to Singapore in January 1856. He left his assistant Charles Allen behind as he was 'of a religious turn' and had decided to train and teach at the Anglican Mission in Kuching. However, in his place, he recruited a fifteen-year-old Malay boy named Ali who had already proved himself a good shot and a useful apprentice. In Singapore, Wallace had to finalise all his specimens for shipment and he sent five thousand insects, including fifteen hundred moths, numerous butterflies, as well as his orangutan skins and skeletons, to Samuel Stevens in London.

With no response from the scientific community regarding his 'Sarawak Paper', Wallace decided to write directly to Charles Darwin in the hope of starting a long distance conversation about his ideas and perhaps even draw Darwin into a conjectural explanation of his observations on the Galapagos Islands. It took many months for Darwin to reply and even more months for his letter to reach Wallace, who was now somewhere out in the islands and jungles of the Indonesian Archipelago.

13

Where Australia Collides with Asia

Alfred Russel Wallace had planned to travel to Macassar in the Celebes (Sulawesi), but unable to find a direct passage, he sailed from Singapore in a schooner bound for Bali and Lombok. The *Kembang Djepoon* (Rose of Japan) was representative of multicultural Singapore since it had a Chinese owner, a Malay name, a Javanese crew and an English Captain. It took twenty days to sail the Java Sea and reach the north coast of Bali, where Wallace was delighted by the views of terraced rice fields and astonished by the highly cultivated nature of the land and its intricate irrigation systems. He wrote that in such a well-cultivated country, he did not expect to do much natural history and he only had two days to do some collecting before the *Kembang Djepoon* sailed on for the port of Ampenam in Lombok. Significantly, the bird species he saw in Bali were those he already knew, such as the Asian Golden Weaver, wagtail-thrushes, orioles and starlings. But in Lombok, it was a different matter, and as he wrote in *The Malay Archipelago*:

> During the few days which I stayed on the north coast of Bali, on my way to Lombok, I saw several birds highly char-

acteristic of Javanese ornithology ... On crossing over to Lombok, separated from Bali by a strait less than twenty miles wide, I naturally expected to meet with some of these birds again; but during a stay of three months I never saw one of them, but found a totally different set of species, most of which were entirely unknown not only in Java, but also in Borneo, Sumatra and Malacca. For example, among the commonest birds in Lombok were white cockatoos and honeysuckers, belonging to family groups which are entirely absent from the western region of the archipelago.

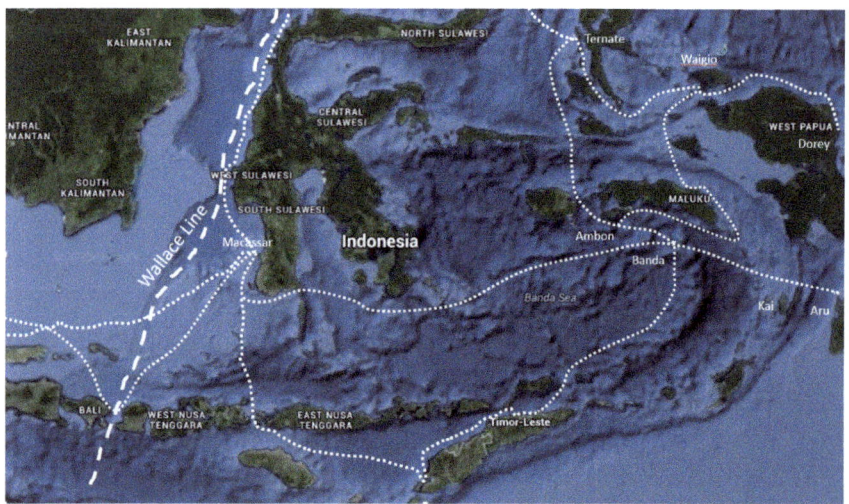

Map showing the Wallace Line and some of his travels around the eastern Indonesian archipelago, Ian Burnet

This was an amazing discovery. The islands of Bali and Lombok are almost identical in terms of soil, climate and position in the archipelago, but belong to two distinct zoological provinces. During the lowering of sea levels during the various Ice Ages, the main Indonesian islands of Sumatra, Java and Borneo were connected by dry land, and it is only the deep Lombok Strait that separates these main islands from the smaller islands to the east. The Lombok Strait represents the biogeographical boundary between the fauna of Asia and that of Australasia, a boundary which Thomas Huxley later named the Wallace Line. We only have to look at a seafloor map now to realise that this Line represents the edge of the Asian continental shelf.

On the Asian side of the Wallace Line are the Asian elephant, the rare Javanese rhinoceros, Sumatran tigers, Borneo leopards, the orangutans of Sumatra and Borneo, and numerous birds that are specific to Asia. On the Australasian side are the white cockatoos and other birds specific to Australia such as the megapodes or scrub turkeys which build large mounds in which they incubate their eggs, the marsupials such as the possum-like cuscus, the tree kangaroos, and the spectacular Birds of Paradise found in Papua and the Moluccas (Maluku). It is no surprise that no megapodes exist west of Lombok, as they had evolved on a continent that was mostly devoid of mammalian carnivores. How long could a ground-living bird survive on a forest floor occupied by tigers or leopards?

Land exposed during the lowering of sea levels during the ice ages allowed Australian flora and fauna to be distributed across the eastern Indonesian islands, except as far as the deep Lombok Strait and its extension north between Borneo and Sulawesi – the Wallace Line. By his observations, Alfred Russel Wallace had invented a new science, the science of biogeography, or the relationship between zoology and geography, as he describes these two divisions of the earth as differing in animal life as Europe does from America.

The earth's surface consists of two kinds of material, the heavier oceanic crust, which is a skin of semi-molten rock connected to the earth's upper mantle, and the lighter continental crust, which 'floats' on the oceanic crust like scum on the surface of a pond. Driven by huge convection currents within the earth's upper mantle, the oceanic crust is broken into a number of separate plates that are in motion. There is no evidence that the earth is expanding, so where new oceanic material is being formed along the mid-ocean ridges, oceanic material is also being consumed along subduction zones around the world. For example, new oceanic crust is being created along the mid-ocean ridge between Australia and Antarctica, and as the oceanic crust and its overlying Australia-New Guinea Continent moves north then oceanic material is being consumed in the subduction zone along the south coast of Java.

Twenty million years ago, or in Miocene times, the incredible northern voyage of the Australian Continent from the Antarctic towards the Equator slows down as it starts to collide with Asia. The Australian Continent which includes Papua-New Guinea, first sweeps aside parts of the Indonesian island arc that stands in its way and then crashes into the Pacific Oceanic plate, locking the two plates together. The Pacific Ocean plate is moving slowly westward, resulting in great chunks of the Australia-New Guinea Continent being sliced off by transcurrent faults and creating the Sulu spur, which has been inserted into the Indonesian island arc system and causing it to bend back upon itself. Lands that had been separated for 200 million years since the northern mega-continent of Laurasia separated from the southern mega-continent of Gondwanaland, now came back together.

While the Pacific Ocean Plate and the Australian Plate are locked onto each other, the Australian Plate continues to move northward. This continuing collision causes large parts of Papua-New Guinea that were once in shallow seas to be thrust upwards, and with further stress to be thrust over the top of each other to form the vast mountains in the Papuan Fold Belt. Mountains such as Mount Puncak Jaya, which at 5000 metres is so high that a tropical glacier still exists on its flanks. Tectonic activity related to this thrusting and uplift includes the emplacement of magmas bearing copper and gold, such as now found at the Grasberg and Porgera gold mines in Papua and New Guinea.

It was not until 1912, fifty years after Wallace first arrived in the Malay Archipelago, that Alfred Wegener proposed his theory of Continental Drift. Although Wegener's theory was not accepted by most geologists at the time, it was quickly accepted by the Dutch geologists working in the East Indies because they saw the folded mountains of northern New Guinea as a collision zone, and collision was the only explanation for the way the islands of the Moluccas (Maluku) had been bent back upon themselves.

Relief map showing the collision of Australia with Asia. Land elevation based on NASA radar topography, sea bathymetry based on NASA satellite altimetry and ship soundings. University of California, San Diego

The first of the Dutch geologists to accept Wegener's theory was Molengraaff, followed by Smit Sibinga who wrote:

> The small Sunda Islands, Celebes and the Moluccas represent marginal chains originally cut off from the Sunda land mass; at first they formed an ordinary double chain, but afterwards took on their present shape due to a collision with the Australian continent.

The uplift of the mountains in Papua-New Guinea pushed remnants of the rainforests of Gondwanaland into higher and wetter altitudes, preserving them and their related plants and animals. Papua-New Guinea's highland forests are a living museum because they provide a home for the Australian marsupials such as the possums, the cuscus, the bandicoots and the echidnas, similar to the way they lived 20 million years ago.

A Goodfellow Tree Kangaroo in Papua New Guinea

One marsupial group has followed a unique evolutionary path, because it is in Papua-New Guinea that the Tree Kangaroo appears to have made the transition back to the arboreal life of its possum-like ancestors. There are no longer any grasses on the forest floor, the most succulent leaves are in the trees and even though they are still clumsy climbers they are able to make their way carefully through the treetops. Having already lost their prehensile tails and opposable thumbs, the tree kangaroos have developed granulated soles on their feet and powerful claws to help them grip branches while they feed on the leaves and fruits of rainforest trees.

Papua-New Guinea is the land of the Birds of Paradise. The plumes adorning the male birds are there because it is the females who choose the most flamboyant of the males to mate with and whose bright colours and array of ribbons, fans, streamers and fur demonstrate how female choice can drive evolution. For the same reason the men of the Highlands paint their bodies and wear these same plumes to attract females, and in their festivities they dance and prance in a manner shared with the Birds of Paradise.

Papua-New Guinea is now the main home of Australia's rainforest birds because here they have a better evolutionary future compared to the small and isolated 'islands' of rainforests that remain in mainland Australia. The relatives of the Papua-New Guinean Birds of Paradise living in the Australian rainforests include the darkly iridescent Trumpet Manucode, and the Paradise Riflebird which, with a glittering turquoise chest and crown, spreads his glistening black wings like an oriental fan when performing his courtship dance. According to Wallace:

> The two most remarkable ... groups of fruit-eating birds – the Parrots and the Pigeons – attain their maximum development as regards beauty, variety, and number of species, in the same limited district, of which the great island of New Guinea forms the centre, and which I have proposed to call the Austro-Malayan subregion.

It is important to note that what Wallace termed the Austro-Malayan subregion, is now named Wallacea in his honour.

Of the shared rainforest plants, botanists conclude that the eastward migration of Asian flora into Papua New Guinea has been more successful, as Asian species such as the Dipterocarp trees, which dominate the tropical Asian rainforest, are found in New Guinea but not in Australia. The westward migration of Australian species, which had already adapted to an arid environment, were less successful at readapting to the tropics. However, an exception might be the clove tree (Myrtacea Syzygium), which has eucalyptus shaped buds, as well as the Melaleuca trees growing on the islands of Manipa and Buru, which are clearly of an Australian origin.

The area of Sulawesi and Maluku, scientifically known as Wallacea, is a curious melange of Asian continental fragments, parts of the Indonesian island arc system, and fragments of the Australian continent moved westward by the Pacific Plate. For example, the islands of Ceram, Manipa and Buru are understood to be continental fragments broken off from Australia. Some of these pieces have been shoved together to create strange hybrid land forms, such as the island of Sulawesi, of which the western half is considered to be part of ancient Laurasia, the eastern half is considered to be part of ancient Gondwanaland, and is there also part of Africa?

All of this caused Alfred Russel Wallace much consternation when he tried to understand the unusual animal assemblage on Sulawesi.

14

Wallace's Voyage to Aru Island

From Lombok, Wallace secured passage on a small schooner for the voyage northward towards Sulawesi (Celebes) and its main town of Macassar. This was the first predominantly Dutch town that he visited in the East Indies, and he found it prettier and cleaner than any he had seen elsewhere in the East:

> The Dutch have some admirable local regulations. All European houses must be kept well whitewashed, and every person must, at four in the afternoon, water the road in front of his house. The streets are kept clear of refuse and covered drains carry away all the impurities ... The town consists chiefly of one long, narrow street along the seaside, devoted to business, and principally occupied by the Dutch and Chinese merchants' offices and warehouses, and the native shops or bazaars ... This street is usually thronged with a native population of Bugis or Macassan men wearing cotton trousers about twelve inches long, covering from the hip to halfway down the thigh, and the universal Malay sarong, of gay checked colours, worn around the waist or across the shoulders in a variety of ways.

**The Malay kampong in Macassar, C.W.M.Van Velde,
Gezigten uit Neerlands Indie**

Wallace settled in a village outside Macassar where he soon learned that not a single person could speak more than a few words of Malay and hardly anyone had seen a European before. The disagreeable part of this was that he excited terror wherever he went. Dogs barked, children screamed, women ran away, and men stared as if he were some strange monster. He describes how pack-horses and buffaloes on the roads were startled by his appearance and if he came upon a well where women were drawing water, or children bathing, a sudden flight was the certain result, 'All of which were very unpleasant to a person who does not like to be disliked, and who had never been accustomed to be treated like an ogre'.

What Wallace found in the forests outside Macassar was astounding because there were hardly any insects, hardly any beetles and very few butterflies. Only the birds seemed a little more promising, but he found no barbets, no trogons, no broadbills, and no shrikes such as he had seen in Singapore, Malaya or Borneo. He wrote that whole families and genera were altogether absent and there is nothing to take their place. Moving further inland he found that:

> While the Celebes is poor in the actual number of species, it is yet wonderfully rich in peculiar forms; many of which are singular or beautiful, and in some cases absolutely unique upon the globe.

In biogeographical terms, Sulawesi has a central position in the Indonesian archipelago and Wallace expected to find a rich diversity of wildlife, but with a land area double that of Java, it had half the number of mammals and land birds. To his surprise, he found that Sulawesi was the poorest in the number of its species and the most isolated in the character of its species compared to all of the great islands of Indonesia:

> The position of the Celebes is the most central in the Archipelago ... Such being the case, we should naturally expect that the productions of this central island in some degree represented the richness and variety of the whole Archipelago ... As so often happens in nature, however, the fact turns out to be the reverse of what we should of expected; and an examination of its animal production shows Celebes to be at once the poorest in the number of its species and the most isolated in the character of its productions of the great islands of the Archipelago ... in proportion to the species which inhabit it far fewer seem derived from other islands, while far more are altogether peculiar to it; and a considerable number of its animal forms are so remarkable, as to find no close allies in any other part of the world.

The endemic animals of Sulawesi such as the crested black macaque, the bizarre Babirusa and the cow-like anoa are more related to Africa than Asia or Australia. The Babirusa is an odd animal since the tusks of its upper jaw instead of growing downwards in the usual way, are completely reversed, growing upward and out of bony sockets through the skin on each side of the snout, curving backwards to near the eyes and in the mature animals often reaching eight or ten inches in length. Another animal unique to Sulawesi and perhaps the strangest is the spectral tarsier, since it is one of the world's smallest primates being only ten centimetres long. Because they are nocturnal they have enormous eyes compared to their body size, and unusually for a primate, they feed only on insects. This was the first of four visits Wallace made to this peculiar terrain and Sulawesi continued to puzzle him:

> The Celebes must be one of the oldest parts of the Archipelago. It probably dates from a period not only anterior to that when Borneo, Java and Sumatra were separated from the continent, but from that still more remote epoch when the land that now constitutes these islands had not risen above the ocean. Such an antiquity is necessary, to account for the number of animal forms it possesses, which show no relation to those of India or Australia, but rather with those of Africa; and we are led to speculate on the possibility of there having once existed a continent in the Indian Ocean which might serve as a bridge to connect these distant countries.

Macassan traders made annual voyages to the Aru Islands in the eastern extremity of the Indonesian archipelago to collect pearl shell, trepang or dried sea slug, and most importantly, bird of paradise skins. For collectors, a bird of paradise specimen was worth more than any other bird on the planet and their skins were traded across the world from Macassar. It was a thousand mile voyage in a native boat, the Bugis prahu, a boat which had made the Macassan traders famous on their annual voyages to the eastern islands and as far south as Arnhem Land in Australia to collect trepang for the Chinese markets.

The Macassans followed the monsoonal winds, leaving in December or January at the beginning of the western monsoon and returning in July or August at the onset of the eastern monsoon, in a voyage that took them away from home for nine months. For the Macassans, this annual voyage to the Aru Islands was looked upon as a rather wild and romantic expedition, full of novel sights and strange adventures.

**Coastal traders from Macassar, Francois-Edmond Paris,
Le Voyage de la Favorite 1830-1832**

For Wallace, it was the lure of the Bird of Paradise that had brought him to the archipelago in the first place and here was an opportunity to reach their distant lands. Despite his trepidation, it was a lure he could not resist:

When I found that I really could do so now, had I but the courage to trust myself for a thousand miles voyage in a Bugis prahu, and then for six or seven months among lawless traders and ferocious savages. I felt somewhat as I did as a schoolboy.

The Bugis prahu is in part a copy of a Western schooner of the mid-nineteenth century, which traded around the archipelago during that period and has been described many times in books by the ship's captain and author, Joseph Conrad. It is built without a nail or any iron being used. Its shipwrights use only an axe, handsaw, adze and auger to shape and fit the ribs and planks of its hull in a time-honoured tradition. The boats are built organically, according to the nature of the timber, and according to a plan that is only in the mind of its master builder, and Wallace wrote that the best European shipwrights could not produce sounder or closer-fitting joints.

To Wallace's untutored eye, the vessel appeared as a wilderness of masts, yards and spars of wood or bamboo, lashed together with rattan. The captain was Dutch-Javanese, and the crew of thirty would have been a mixture of Macassan, Bugis and Javanese. According to Wallace, there did not appear to be any distinct chain of command, yet everyone seemed willing enough to work. There were usually half a dozen voices giving orders and he writes that in such shrieking and confusion, it seems wonderful that anything gets done at all.

Wallace brought with him an eight-month supply of necessities - sugar, coffee, tea, a keg of butter, sixteen flasks of oil, cooking utensils, lamps and candles, as well as luxuries such as a dozen bottles of wine and some beer. His hunting and collecting supplies consisted of guns, bags of shot, gunpowder, insect boxes, pins, preserving alcohol, as well as tobacco, beads and *parang* (machetes) for trading. He was accompanied by his trusty assistant Ali whom he had met in Sarawak and two young men hired in Macassar. Wallace commandeered the small bamboo and thatch cabin on deck which he described as 'the snuggest and most comfortable little place I have ever enjoyed at sea'. The light filtering through the bamboo walls and the natural smell of the thatch allowed him to recall quiet scenes in a green and shady forest. At night the stars hung bright in the sky above and it was a magical sight to look down into the water and see streams of phosphorescent light as thousands of bio-luminescent organisms swirl and light up in its wake. Something which Wallace describes as resembling 'One of the large, irregular, nebulous star-clusters seen through a good telescope, with the additional attraction of an ever changing form and dancing motion'.

The Banda Islands, Louis Le Breton, Navires par Mayer

The Banda Islands were their first landfall after crossing the Banda Sea and a convenient stopping point to take on water and supplies. These tiny islands seem to be formed by the rim of a remnant volcano, which rises 5000 metres from the depths of the Banda Sea. Wallace walked up a pretty path to the highest point of the island behind the small town of Banda Neira. From here, he had a perfect view across to the new volcano called Gunung Api or 'Fire Mountain', which has a pyramidal shape. This was the first time that Wallace was able to closely observe a volcano. He commented that most people of northern Europe viewed the earth as a symbol of stability, whereas a volcano is opposite to this learned experience. He noted that it is only when gazing on an active volcano that one can fully realise the mighty forces of the interior of the earth and from whence comes that inexhaustible fire that produces its smoking peak:

> The volcano first appearing – a perfect cone, having much the outline of the Egyptian pyramids, and looking almost as regular. In the evening the smoke rested over its summit like a small stationary cloud. This was my first view of an active volcano, but pictures and panoramas have so impressed such things on one.

It was Portuguese explorers who were the first Europeans to reach the Banda Islands in 1512. They had come in search of the valuable nutmeg spice that had been traded for centuries by Javanese, Malays, Indians, Arabs and Persians across vast oceans and vast deserts until they reached the Mediterranean Sea and the European spice markets. One hundred years after the Portuguese began their trading empire, the Dutch and English East India Companies arrived in the Banda Islands seeking their share of profits from this valuable trade. The English and the Dutch East India Companies were founded in 1601 and 1602 respectively to profit from the trade in spices and these were the world's first joint stock companies. It was the Dutch who dominated over their rivals and after they virtually eliminated the population of the Banda Islands by the 'Banda Massacre', the Dutch East India Company was then able to establish its colony of Dutch plantation owners and enslaved workers to cultivate the nutmeg trees and reap huge profits from their nutmeg monopoly.

Banda Neira was an administrative capital for the Dutch East India Company (VOC) and even today there are reminders of its colonial past. The whitewashed governor's residence has some classical architectural features, from the golden lions mounted on the entrance gates, to the now defunct fountain on the lawn in the forecourt, to the elegant simplicity of the four columns on the terrace and the symmetry of its shuttered doors and windows. Broad avenues are lined by once grand homes, the once elegant and now dilapidated Dutch Club, all cast an air of forlorn former grandeur over the town.

The Banda Islands are rimmed by coconut palms and covered by an evergreen forest of nutmeg trees and the larger kenari shade trees that protect them from the harsh tropical sun. These remote islands are the only place in the world where commercial nutmegs originally grew and it is a mystery how the nutmeg tree came to these islands in the middle of the vast Banda Sea. Yet there are native nutmegs growing in North Queensland in Australia, so how are these two connected and which nutmegs came first? Alfred Russel Wallace describes the nutmeg trees on the Banda Islands:

> Few cultivated plants are more beautiful than the nutmeg trees. They are handsomely shaped and glossy leaved, growing to a height of 8 metres bearing small yellowish flowers. The fruit is the size and colour of a peach, but rather oval. It is of a tough fleshy consistence but when ripe splits open and shows the dark nut within, covered with crimson mace, and is then a most beautiful object. Within the hard shell of the nut is the seed, which is the nutmeg of commerce. The nuts are eaten by the large pigeons of Banda, which digest the mace but cast up the nut, with its seed uninjured.

When the nutmeg is ripe, it splits open to reveal the mace, which is a crimson net wrapped around the shiny dark brown seed, which contains the actual nutmeg. Both the mace and the nutmeg are simply dried for a day in the sun and are then ready for export. Wallace was excited to observe the white and lilac-blue flashes of the huge nutmeg pigeons, which feed exclusively on the nutmeg fruit and can open their beak wide enough to swallow and digest the complete fruit, which is itself the size of a small peach. They pass the seed to grow where it falls and it is probably these pigeons that first brought the nutmegs from these remote islands to Northern Australia, or is it the other way around?

The next stopping point for the Macassans were the Kai islands, and a map shows these are near the hinge point where the islands of Maluku have been bent back upon themselves after the collision of Australia-New Guinea with this part of the island arc. Ever since his time on the Rio Negro and his first encounter with the Baniwa people, Alfred Russel Wallace had become something of an anthropologist as well as a naturalist, as he carefully observed and recorded the habits of the native people he encountered during his travels. He also recorded their languages, and during his travels in the archipelago, he collected the vocabulary from fifty-seven distinct regional languages, as well as the common Malay and Javanese languages. After spending the three previous years living amongst the Malay people who populate most of the archipelago. His first encounter with the Papuans, with their darker skin, frizzy hair and different character, was on arriving at Kai. He describes how he could have been blind and still be certain that he had entered a new world, inhabited by a different race of people:

> The loud, rapid, eager tones, the incessant motion, the intense vital activity manifested in speech and action are the very antipodes of the quiet, unimpulsive, unanimated Malay. These Kai men came up singing and shouting, dipping their paddles deep in the water and throwing up clouds of spray; as they approached nearer, they stood up in their canoes and increased their noise and gesticulations: and on coming alongside, without asking leave, and without a moment's hesitation, the greater part of them scrambled up on our deck just as if they were to take possession of a captured vessel ... These forty black, naked,

mop-headed savages seemed intoxicated with joy and excitement. Not one of them could remain still for a moment.

Wallace provides an amusing anecdote of himself, from a different race of people, being observed by a villager when he was collecting insects on Kai. He describes how an elderly man carefully observed this strange, tall, bearded, bespectacled species of European man collect an insect, then, neatly skewer its exoskeleton with a pin and as if carrying out a ritual, place the specimen in a little wooden box. The bemused old man stood very quietly watching this spectacle, when, as Wallace describes it, 'he could contain himself no longer, but bent almost double, and enjoyed a hearty roar of laughter'.

Despite his initial trepidation when first contemplating this voyage, Wallace declared that he had never, either before or since, made a twenty day voyage so pleasantly, or with so little discomfort, and he wrote:

> I was much delighted with the trip, and was inclined to rate the luxuries of the semi-barbarous prahu as surpassing those of the most magnificent screw-steamer, that highest result of our civilisation.

At the end of their long voyage, they reached the trading settlement of Dobbo, which is just off the coast of the main island of Aru. It consisted of three rows of thatched houses or large sheds for the Bugis and Chinese traders who came there and built out on a sand spit with a sheltered anchorage on either side. Wallace quickly found a house, installed a bamboo bench for a bed, a cane chair and table, some shelves for his supplies, and declared himself as contented as if he had found a well-furnished mansion.

The main population of the Aru Islands are dark, frizzy-haired Melanesians and even darker frizzy-haired Papuans, or their derivatives. However, during the trading season when Wallace was there,

Dobbo attracted nearly five hundred people of many different races. There were Chinese, Macassan, Bugis, Ceramese, and men from the other eastern islands, many of whom had a reputation of dishonesty and immorality. Wallace goes on to describe how this motley, ignorant, bloodthirsty and thievish population came to live here without the shadow of any government, with no police, no courts and no lawyers. He concludes that trade is the magic that keeps them all at peace and unites these discordant elements into a well-behaved community. Like Wallace, these men had travelled large distances to be in Dobbo during the trading season. They knew that peace and order are essential for successful trade and any lawlessness was quickly settled amongst themselves for the common good.

There was no Dutch presence on these remote islands and Wallace was the only white man in the settlement. For obvious reasons he became a curiosity and he describes his many visits from the locals:

> This was the first time a real white man had come among them, and, they said, "You see how the people come every day from the villages around to look at you", This was very flattering, and accounted for the great concourse of visitors which I had at first imagined was accidental. A few years before I had been one of the gazers at the Zulus and the Aztecs in London. Now the tables were turned on me, for I was to these people a new and strange variety of man, and I had the honour of affording to them, in my own person, an attractive exhibition.

On Wallace's first day exploring the forest on Wamma, he collected thirty species of butterfly, including many rare and beautiful varieties which had only been previously known by a few specimens from New Guinea. The following two days were wet and windy, but on the succeeding day he had the good fortune to capture one of the most magnificent insects in the world, the Great Bird-Winged Butterfly or *Ornithoptera poseidon*:

The great birdwing butterfly or Ornthoptera priamus poseidon

I trembled with excitement as I saw it coming majestically toward me, and could hardly believe I had really succeeded in my stroke till I had taken it out of the net and was gazing, lost in admiration, at the velvet black and brilliant green of its wings, seven inches across, its golden body, and crimson breast. It is true I had seen similar insects in cabinets, at home, but it is quite another thing to capture such one's self – to feel it struggling between one's fingers, and to gaze upon its fresh and living beauty, a bright gem shining out amid the silent gloom of a dark and tangled forest. The village of Dobbo held that evening at least one contented man.

The first specimens of birds of paradise to arrive in Europe came with the Portuguese explorers. Those early explorers who reached the Moluccan Islands were shown skins of the brightly coloured and richly decorated birds. For some reason, these first specimens were legless, and they came with a story that the birds never landed, but mated and hatched their eggs in a heavenly paradise. It was in 1522 that the *Victoria*, the only ship of Ferdinand Magellan's fleet to complete the first circumnavigation of the world, returned to Spain with two bird of paradise skins given by the Sultan of Bacan as a gift for the King of Spain. As written by Antonio Pigafetta the chronicler of their voyage:

> He also gave for the King of Spain two most beautiful dead birds … They have no wings but instead of them long feathers of different colours, like plumes … They never fly, except when

the wind blows. The people told us that those birds come from the terrestrial paradise, and they call them *bolon diuata*, that is to say, Birds of God.

Wallace was disappointed that he had not yet seen any birds of paradise on Wamma, but soon learned that at this time of the year they were all out of plumage. However, the small red species, the King Bird of Paradise, retained its plumage all year round so if he could get across to the main island of Aru he might still find some. This voyage across the narrow straits was delayed because of the threat of pirates:

> Just as I was trying to arrange a trip to the larger island, a fleet of Magindano pirates made their appearance, committing great devastations, and putting the whole place in an uproar; and it was only after they had been sometime gone that confidence began to be restored, and the natives could be persuaded to take the smallest voyage. This delayed me two months in Dobbo without seeing a Paradise bird.

The Magindano pirates came from the Sulu Archipelago south of the Philippines and made regular raids on small unprotected settlements in the eastern Indonesian Archipelago, where they carried off what they could, including women and children, and then escaped in their well-manned prahus to hide on some uninhabited island and prepare for their next raid. One evening after Wallace had crossed over to Aru and reached his base at Wanumbai, he heard the cry of "Bajak! Bajak!" (Pirates! Pirates!) The villagers all rushed down to the beach with their weapons, but it proved to be a false alarm and was only their comrades returning from a fishing trip:

> When all was quiet again, one of the men, who could speak a little Malay, came to me and begged me not to sleep too hard. "Why?" I asked. "Perhaps the pirates may really come", he said

very seriously, which made me laugh and assure him I should sleep as hard as I could.

For Wallace sleeping here was hard, as ants, spiders, centipedes and scorpions all shared his hut. The collecting was poor but after two or three days, one of his assistants returned with a jewel, the King Bird of Paradise, a bird that no European had seen in the wild. This is what Wallace had come so far to see and he was ecstatic:

**The King bird of Paradise, Cicinnurus regius,
J.Wolf and J.Smit, Biodiversity Library**

The King Bird of Paradise when first brought to me exacted greater admiration and delight than I have experienced on any similar occasion. It was a small bird, a little less than a thrush. The greater part of its plumage was of an intense cinnabar red, with a gloss of spun glass ... Merely in arrangement of colours and texture of plumage this little bird was a gem of the first order, yet these comprised only half of its strange beauty ... Two ornaments, the breast-fans and the spiral-tipped tail-wires, are altogether unique, not occurring on any other species of the eight thousand different birds that are known to exist upon the earth; and, combined with the most exquisite beauty of plumage, render this one of the most perfectly lovely of the many lovely productions of nature. My admiration and delight quite amused my Aru hosts, who saw nothing more in the 'burung raja' than we see in the robin or goldfinch.

It was four months later that Wallace was first able to see the Great Bird of Paradise in full plumage with its long trains of silky feathers. Lying in his hut before dawn, he awoke to their cries as they went to seek their breakfast. The mating season had begun, and he observed their extravagant 'dance parties', conducted to win the watching female birds. As they danced, the males raised their tails into magnificent golden fans, shook these quivering fans, and then froze like an open flower, before quivering again. Wallace was the first European to see the elaborate courtship dances of these birds, he now knew that the Bird of Paradise really deserves its name and must be ranked as one of the most beautiful and most wonderful of all living things:

> The birds had now commenced dancing parties, in certain trees in the forest … On one of these trees a dozen or twenty full-plumaged male birds assemble together, raise up their wings, stretch out their necks, and elevate their exquisite plumes, keeping them in a continual vibration … so that the whole tree is filled with waving plumes in every variety of attitude and motion. The bird itself is nearly as large as a crow, and is of a rich brown colour. The head and the neck is of a pure straw yellow above, and rich metallic green beneath. The long plumy tufts of golden orange feathers spring from the sides beneath each wing, and when the bird is in repose are partly concealed by them.

To collect the Great Birds of Paradise, the Aru islanders built hides in the lower branches of the trees close to where the male birds performed their 'dance parties'. From here, they could shoot their arrows tipped with a blunt head that would stun or kill the bird without damaging the valuable feathers. Although Wallace himself was a collector and planned to take away as many specimens of these magnificent birds as he could, the beauty of these birds aroused contradictory thoughts within him, and he was farsighted enough to see what might be the future of many rare and endangered species:

The Greater Bird of Paradise,
Paradisaea Apoda
J.Wolf and J.Smit, Biodiversity Library

It seems sad that on the one hand such exquisite creatures should live out their lives and exhibit their charms only in these wild and inhospitable regions ... while on the other hand, should civilized man ever reach these distant lands, and bring moral, intellectual and physical light into the recesses of these virgin forests, we may be sure that he will so disturb the nicely balanced relations of organic and inorganic nature as to cause the disappearance, and finally the extinction, of these very beings whose wonderful structure and beauty he alone is fitted to appreciate and enjoy. This consideration must surely tell us that all living things were 'not' made for man.

Returning to Dobbo with his prize specimens Wallace found that the town was now full of traders and he had to find temporary accommodation in what was called the 'courthouse'. For six weeks he was confined indoors while his feet healed from sand-fly bites that had swelled up and become infected. He spent his time writing up his notes and preparing his specimens for shipment. He had a total of nine thousand specimens of which about sixteen hundred were distinct species and worth a fortune in London. The Macassan traders were now loading their prahus for the return voyage on the east monsoonal winds, and he would sail with them back to Macassar with his treasures. During his time in Aru, Wallace had made the acquaintance of a strange and little-known race of men, he had become familiar with the archipelago traders, had revelled in the delights of exploring a new flora and fauna, and had been able to view the magnificent Great Birds of Paradise performing their 'dancing parties' in their native forests.

On the return voyage to Macassar, sitting in his small bamboo and thatch cabin while working on his notes, Wallace had plenty of time to consider what he had observed. He knew that the Birds of Paradise, along with the other birds on Aru were also found in New Guinea. He noted the similarities between the fauna of Aru and New Guinea, and the fauna of New Guinea and Australia. Apart from bats (which migrate long distances) and pigs (introduced by man) all the mammals he found on Aru were marsupials, such as the Dusky Pademelon or Aru Island Wallaby, which together with the cockatoos, cassowaries and brush turkeys are typically Australian fauna and he wrote:

> The fact of the Aru Islands having once been connected to New Guinea does not rest on this evidence alone. There is such a striking resemblance between the productions of the two countries as only exists between portions of a common territory. I collected one hundred species of land-birds in the Aru Islands, and about eighty of them have been found on the mainland of New Guinea. Among these are the great wingless cassowary, two species of heavy brush turkeys, and two of short-winged thrushes, which could certainly not have passed over 150 miles of open sea from the coast of New Guinea ... Again a true

kangaroo is found in Aru ... and another small marsupial animal (*Perameles doreyanus*) is common to Aru and New Guinea.

Wallace could not help but be intrigued by the similarities of the native fauna of Aru to that of New Guinea and of them both to Australian fauna. Of course we now know that New Guinea and Aru carry Australian fauna because they were always part of the Australian continent and although they now stand above sea level as wrinkles on its continental margin they were certainly connected during the lowering of sea levels in the different ice ages.

Back in Macassar, Wallace prepared a paper to send to London for the *Annals and Magazine of Natural History* entitled *On the Natural History of the Aru Islands*. His paper, published in 1857, suggested that these islands had once been connected to New Guinea by a land bridge and subsequently separated by rising seas. In trying to describe the differences between Asia and Australia, Wallace used the examples of Borneo and Papua-New Guinea since these two great islands are similar in climate and terrain, are rich in tropical tree species, yet their faunas are completely different, while by contrast Papua-New Guinea and Australia have completely different climates and terrain yet their fauna are similar:

> Borneo and New Guinea, as alike physically as two distinct countries can be, are as zoologically different as the poles are asunder. While Australia, with its dry winds, its open plains, its stony deserts, and its temperate climate, yet produces birds and quadrupeds which are closely related to those inhabiting the hot damp, luxuriant forests which everywhere clothe the plains and mountains of New Guinea.
>
> In order to illustrate more clearly the means by which I suppose this great contrast has been brought about, let us consider what would occur if two strongly-contrasted divisions of the earth were, by natural means, brought into proximity. No two

parts of the world differ so radically in their productions as Asia and Australia.

Fifty years before Alfred Wegener first published his theory of Continental Drift and one hundred years before the modern understanding of Plate Tectonics, Alfred Russel Wallace had concluded from his observations of the zoology of the eastern archipelago that Australia had collided with Asia.

15

Alfred Russel Wallace - The 'Letter from Ternate'

On Wallace's return to Macassar after a nine month absence in Aru he found a pile of mail waiting for him. This included a letter from Charles Darwin dated May 1, 1857 related to the publication of Wallace's 'Sarawak Law' and his indirect challenge to Darwin to provide at least a 'conjectural explanation' for his observations in the Galapagos Islands. Darwin wrote:

> I can plainly see that we have thought much alike and to a certain extent have come to similar conclusions. In regard to your paper in the Annals, I agree to the truth of almost every word ... and I daresay that you will agree with me that it is very rare to find oneself agreeing pretty closely with any theoretical paper. This summer will mark the 20th year (!) since I have opened my first note-book, on the question how and in what way do species and varieties differ from each other. – I am now preparing my work for publication, but I find the subject so very large, that though I have written many chapters, I do not suppose I shall go to press for two years ... It is really impossible to explain my views in the compass of a letter on the

causes and means of variation in a state of nature; but I have slowly adopted a distinct and tangible idea. – Whether true or false others must judge ... You say that you have been somewhat surprised at no notice having been taken of your paper in the Annals: I cannot say that I am; for so few naturalists care for anything beyond the mere description of species. But you must not suppose that your paper has not been attended to: two very good men, Sir C. Lyell and Mr E. Blyth at Calcutta specially called my attention to it.

Wallace was excited to receive a letter directly from his boyhood hero including Darwin's recognition and agreement with his 'Sarawak Law'. But in many other ways this was an intriguing letter. Darwin was laying claim to some sort of priority over Wallace by stating that he has been working on this problem for twenty years and expects to publish in the next two years. But there was no 'conjectural explanation' of what Darwin had observed in the Galapagos and he obviously has no intention of revealing any part of his 'big dangerous idea' to Wallace, because, as he says, it is far too complex to explain in a letter.

Later that year Wallace left Macassar on the Dutch mail steamer bound for the Spice Islands and after brief stops on the islands of Timor, Banda and Ambon he arrived at the North Moluccan island of Ternate in January 1858. Life aboard the Dutch steamer must have been pure luxury compared to his usual privations while collecting specimens in the jungle. He took tea or coffee before his 6 am breakfast of eggs and sardines. Madeira or gin and bitters were served on deck before lunch. Before dinner there was gin and bitters, claret or beer, followed after dinner by cigars in the lounge for the men. A final service of tea, coffee and cake around 8pm concluded the day. Wallace described all these as little 'gastronomic excitements' meant to while away the tedium of a long sea voyage towards the Spice Islands:

> I look forward with unmixed satisfaction to my visit to the rich and almost unexplored Spice Islands – the land of the lories, the cockatoos and the birds of paradise, the country of tortoise-shell and pearls, of beautiful shells and rare insects. I look forward with expectation and awe to visiting lands exposed to destruction from the sleeping volcano and its kindred earthquake, and not less do I anticipate the pleasures of observing the varied races of mankind, and becoming familiar with the manners, customs and modes of thought of people so far removed from the European races and European civilisation.

From earliest times, traders sailed from the Spice Islands across vast oceans in leaky boats to bring clove buds and nutmegs to markets in East Africa, the Middle East, India and China. Loaded onto the backs of recalcitrant camels, the spices were transported across the deserts of Egypt, Arabia and Central Asia before finally reaching the Mediterranean Sea and markets in Europe. The length of this journey halfway around the world and the profits and taxes extracted at each stage meant that when demand was highest these simple buds and seeds were said to be worth their weight in gold. After the expansion of Islam across the Middle East in the seventh century, the spice trade was monopolised by the Muslims who were by now the sworn enemies of Christian Europe.

The Pope and the kings of Europe supported those explorers willing to sail into unknown seas in search of a direct route to the Spice Islands and to bring Christianity to the lands they discovered. The voyages of the Portuguese explorers such as Bartholomeu Dias and Vasco da Gama, and the Spanish-backed explorers such as Christopher Columbus and Ferdinand Magellan were an attempt to find a new route to the Indies and the Spice Islands, and it was these epic voyages of 'The Age of Discovery' that allowed mankind to put a definite shape to the oceans and continents of our planet for the first time in human history.

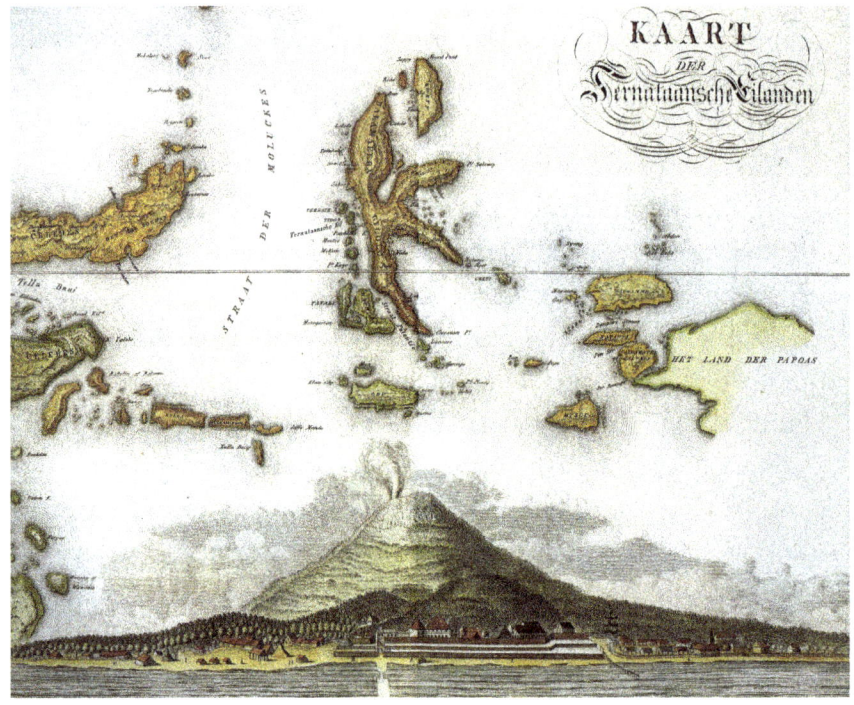

Fort Oranje, Mount Gamalama and Ternate, J.Van den Bosch, 1818

At first the islands might have seemed to be a peaceful and idyllic tropical paradise fanned by a gentle sea breeze scented by exotic spices and with a compliant population that could easily be controlled by a powerful colonial master. However, the Portuguese quickly found themselves embroiled in the rivalry and intrigues from within the Sultan's court and after sixty years Fort Gamalama was captured from the Portuguese by the Sultan of Ternate. The Dutch East India Company defeated the Portuguese in 1606 when they captured the Portuguese fort on the adjacent island of Tidore. They later occupied an abandoned Portuguese fort on the east coast of Ternate and after rebuilding the fort and reinforcing its garrison they renamed it Fort Oranje, and this is the fort that stands in the centre of Ternate today.

In the 1670s the naturalist Georg Rumphius described the clove tree as the most beautiful, the most elegant and the most precious of all known trees. Like most under-story trees, it is unable to regenerate under the full tropical sun and its seed is only viable for a short period, which may explain why its worldwide distribution was limited to these few tiny islands.

A member of the *Myrtacea* family, the clove tree grows to a height of ten metres and is covered with glossy and powerfully aromatic leaves, but it is the flower bud that is valued. The clove buds grow in clusters and change colour as they mature, from green through yellow to pink and finally a deep russet red. In order to retain the maximum amount of their aromatic oil, the buds are harvested before they flower, then spread out on mats to dry. The buds harden and blacken as the heat of the tropical sun seals in their fragrant oil. As the clove bud and stem dries, it takes on the characteristic nail like appearance that gives the spice its name, which is derived from the Latin word *clavus* for nail. Cloves were used by the ancients not just for their unique flavour and aroma, but also for their antibacterial and analgesic properties, which made them highly valued in a world without modern medicine. The fact that it takes more than 3000 flower buds to produce one kilogram of dried cloves may also explain why they are so valuable.

Wallace arrived in Ternate in January 1858 and rented a house from the Dutchman Maarten Duivenbode who was the owner of many ships, plantations and whole districts in the Spice Islands and had become known as the "King of Ternate". The house had four rooms a large hall, verandas front and back, a garden full of fruit trees, a deep well but was in need of some repairs. Five minutes' walk down the road from Wallace's house was the market and the waterfront with its outrigger fishing boats drawn up on the beach. At the waterfront one had beautiful views across the water to the perfect volcanic cone of

Mount Kiematabu on the opposite island of Tidore, with its summit often swathed in cloud.

**View of Mount Kiematabu on the island of Tidore seen from Ternate.
Ian Burnet**

Behind his house rose Mount Gamalama, the volcano that dominated Ternate and threatened to erupt at any time as it smoked, belched and occasionally shook the town. The lower part of the mountain was almost entirely covered with a forest of fruit trees with mangoes, durian, mangosteens and langsat among them and the townsfolk would go up to the orchards every day to gather the fruit which was in season. Here is how Wallace wrote of his residence:

> In Ternate a deep well supplied me with pure cold water – a great luxury in this climate. Five minutes' walk down the road brought me to the market and the beach. In this house I spent many happy days. Returning to it after three or four months'

absence in some uncivilized region. I enjoyed the unwonted luxuries of milk and fresh bread, and regular supplies of fish and eggs, meat and vegetables, which were often sorely needed to restore my health and energy. I had ample space and convenience for unpacking, sorting, and arranging my treasures, and I had delightful walks in the suburbs of the town, or up the lower slopes of the mountain.

Ternate became Wallace's principle residence and his base for the next three years while he took collecting trips to adjacent islands such as Halmahera, Bacan, Ceram, and as far east as Wagio and Papua. There must have been a social life amongst the Dutch officials and colonial residents on the island, but Wallace had become used to his own solitary existence and wrote that when back in Ternate 'I seldom have a visitor but I wish him away in an hour, as I find seclusion very favourable to reflection'.

From Ternate, Wallace crossed the narrow Patinti Strait to the large island of Gilolo or Halmahera as it is now known. Here he rented a hut in the village of Dodinga where he stayed for over a month and obtained a number of insects which were quite new. However, and not for the first time, he fell ill with malaria. Confined to his simple hut he suffered the debilitating cycle of a sudden coldness, followed by shivering, then a fever and sweating to be repeated over many days. In this semi-delirious state ideas would flash before him and then disappear. The question of the origin of species was always on his mind and fortunately there had been a copy of *Principles of Population* by Thomas Malthus in the Leicester town library. As in the case of Charles Darwin, it was Malthus's ideas that provided the breakthrough:

> I was suffering from a rather severe attack of intermittent fever, which prostrated me for several hours every day during the cold and succeeding hot fits. During one of these fits, while again considering the problem of the origin of species, some-

thing brought to my recollection Thomas Malthus's 'Principles of Population', which I had read about twelve years before. I thought of his clear exposition of 'the positive checks to increase' – disease, accidents, war and famine – which kept the populations of savage races to so much lower on average than that of more civilized peoples. It then occurred to me that these causes or their equivalents are continually acting in the case of animals also; and as animals usually breed much more rapidly than does mankind ... Why do some die and some live? And the answer was clearly, that on the whole the best fitted live. From the effects of disease the most healthy escaped; from enemies, the strongest, the swiftest, or the most cunning; from famine, the best hunters or those with the best digestion; and so on. Then it suddenly flashed upon me that this self-acting process would necessarily 'improve the race', because in every generation the inferior would inevitably be killed off and the superior would remain – that is, 'the fittest would survive'.

In particular Wallace had noted that certain beetles always adapted their coloration according to their environment, so they were less conspicuous to predators. According to his theory a beetle, for example, might be produced in many different types of coloration but 'the fittest' in this case the least conspicuous would be most likely survive to reproduce. By this method the superior 'variety' would then expand and could eventually replace its soon to be extinct ancestor:

> Most or perhaps all the variations from the typical form of a species must have some definite effect however slight, on the habits or capacities of the individuals. Even a change of colour might by rendering them more or less distinguishable, affect their safety.

As soon as he had recovered from his malarial fevers, Wallace began making notes of these thoughts and on his return to Ternate he began writing his famous paper entitled *On the Tendency of Varieties to Depart Indefinitely from the Original Type* which he dated Ternate, February, 1858. He remembered the letter he had received from Charles Darwin related to his studies on how species and varieties differ from each other. Surely this was the breakthrough Darwin was looking for:

> The same evening I did this pretty fully, and on two succeeding evenings wrote it out carefully in order to send it to Darwin by the next post, which will leave in a day or two ... I said that I hoped the idea would be as new to him as it was to me, and that it would supply the missing factor to explain the origin of species. I asked him, if he thought it sufficiently important, to show it to Sir Charles Lyell, who had thought so highly of my former paper.

According to Wallace's diary his letter was despatched on March 9, 1858 when a Dutch cargo vessel arrived in Ternate on its regular run around the Moluccas. He paid the captain the amount necessary to transfer the letter to Singapore, from here it was transferred to a British ship bound for Southampton and then delivered to Down House via the mail from London, where on July 18 one of Darwin's servants would have paid the two shillings due in England for unfranked overseas mail.

Would Wallace's idea be as new to Darwin as it was to him? Wallace knew that it would take 3-4 months for his letter to reach Charles Darwin and around the same time for him to receive a response. There was no point in him hanging around Ternate and besides there was the large island of Papua-New Guinea to explore.

16

Alfred Russel Wallace – The Voyage to Wagio

Having come up with his revolutionary idea, *On the Tendency of Varieties to Depart from the Original Type,* Wallace was not going to stand still, as he had long planned an expedition to Papua-New Guinea and its surrounding islands. This was the natural home of the Bird of Paradise, the tree kangaroo and many of the other 'Australian' species that he hoped to find. Knowing the potential difficulties of collecting in this, the remotest part of the Indonesian Archipelago, he wrote:

> I am engaged here in a wider and more general study – that of the relations of animals to time and space, or in other words, their geographical and geological distribution and its causes. I have set myself to work out this problem in the Indo-Australian Archipelago and I must visit and explore the largest number of islands possible and collect animals from the greatest number of localities in order to arrive at any definite results. As to health and life, what are they compared with peace and happiness.

Dorey, on the northwest coast of Papua, was where the French naturalist René Primavère Lesson, from the French expedition vessel *La Coquille*, is believed to have been the first European to see the beautiful birds of paradise in the wild, some thirty years earlier in 1824. Transfixed by the vision of the bird in flight with its colourful plumage and trailing plumes, he apparently forgot that he was meant to shoot and collect, this the most magnificent of all birds, as he wrote:

> Whilst we were walking very carefully on a wild pig trail through the dense scrub ... A *Paradisaea* suddenly flew in graceful curves over my head. It was like a meteor whose body, cutting through the air, leaves a long trail of light. We were so amazed that the flintlocks in our hands did not move.

Arriving at Manokwari Bay on the northwest coast of Papua, Wallace and his four assistants set about building a hut at Dorey that would serve them for the next few months of collecting. When they had finished building, he brought up all his goods and stores and considered himself fairly established as the only European inhabitant of the vast island of Papua-New Guinea. This was the end of the wet season and the whole country was still soaked in water. Food was scarce, and his group was reduced to eating the corpses of the birds they had shot to collect the skins. A single parakeet, Wallace complained, had to serve him for two meals. He describes regularly wading up to his knees in mud and then slicing his ankle while clambering over the trunks and branches of fallen trees. This wound soon turned septic and for several weeks he could not leave his hut, driven to despair. Wallace describes his situation:

> I was tantalized by seeing grand butterflies flying past my door, and thinking of the twenty or thirty new species of insects I ought to be getting every day. And this, too, in New Guinea! – A country which I might never visit again – a country in which

no naturalist had ever resided in before – a country which contained more strange and new and beautiful natural objects than any other part of the globe. The naturalist will be able to appreciate my feelings, sitting from morning to night in my little hut, unable to move without a crutch.

There was, however, a profusion of insects around their hut, and on his best day, he collected 78 distinct sorts of beetles. There was also a very aggressive species of small black ant, which swarmed all over his work table while attempting to carry off his specimens from under his very nose. This was meant to be the dry season, but the rain continued. And there was worse to come, as he and almost all his party were beginning to suffer from fever or dysentery or both. Wallace recovered, but a young man named Jumaat, whom he had brought from Ternate as a shooter, died, and they buried him according to Islamic ritual in a cotton shroud. They were all terribly ill and the death of their friend and compatriot was surely enough to convince them to leave. The trip to Papua was a disaster and Wallace now longed to get away from this place as much as he had ever longed to get there. However, there was no regular shipping service sailing from Dorey. After almost four months of misery, they could finally return by ship to Ternate:

> We bade adieu to Dorey, without much regret, for in no place which I have visited have I encountered more privations and annoyances. Continual rain, continual sickness, little wholesome food, with a plague of ants and flies, surpassing anything I had before met with, required all a naturalist's ardour to encounter; and when they were unaccompanied by great success in collecting, became all the more insupportable. This long-thought-of and much-desired voyage to New Guinea had realised none of my expectations. Instead of being far better than the Aru Islands it was in almost everything much worse.

Instead of producing several of the rarer paradise birds, I had not even seen one of them, and had not obtained even one superlatively fine bird or insect. I could not deny, however, that Dorey was very rich in ants.

Wallace's attempt to find birds of paradise near the coast of New Guinea failed because they were mainly found in the rugged Arfak Mountains, south of Dorey and several weeks journey into the wild interior. The skins that had found their way to Europe for naturalists to examine had been collected by the savage tribes of the interior and then traded from village to village until they reached the coast. Wallace wrote:

> It seems as if Nature had taken precautions that these her choicest treasures should not be made too common, and thus be undervalued ... The country is all rocky and mountainous, covered everywhere with dense forests, offering in its swamps and precipices and serrated ridges an almost impossible barrier to the unknown interior; and the people are dangerous savages, in the very lowest stages of barbarism. In such a country, and among such people, are found these wonderful productions of Nature, the birds of paradise, whose exquisite beauty of form and colour and strange developments of plumage are calculated to excite the wonder and admiration of the most civilised and the most intellectual of mankind.

Some two months after his return to Ternate, Wallace sailed south past the line of volcanoes that form the islands of Tidore, Motir and Makian to the island of Bacian or Bacan, which is the southernmost and largest of the seven Spice Islands that lie off the west coast of the main island of Gilolo or Halmahera. This island has some large mountains, numerous rivers or streams, and the forest appeared to be dense and luxuriant. Wallace hoped there would be a corresponding richness in birds and insects, and during his first walk in the forest, Wallace spotted a butterfly that he recognised as the female of the new species of *Ornithoptera*, the magnificent Golden Birdwing.

Wallace's golden birdwing, *Ornithoptera croesus*

He hoped to find the male, which is extremely beautiful, and the excitement when he succeeded was intense:

> The beauty and brilliancy of this insect are indescribable and none but a naturalist can understand the intense excitement I experienced when at length I captured it. On taking it out of my net and opening the glorious wings, my heart began to beat violently, the blood rushed to my head, and I felt much more like fainting than I have done when in apprehension of immediate death. I had a headache the rest of the day, so great was the excitement by what will appear to most people a very inadequate cause.

The forests of Bacan were soon to reveal another of their secrets and provide Alfred Russel Wallace and his assistant Ali with what he considered to be his greatest collecting achievement.

**Wallace's standardwing, Semioptera wallacai,
John Jennens, 1860**

After a day out collecting insects around some ground being cleared for a new coal mine, Wallace was returning home when he met Ali:

Just as I got home I overtook Ali returning from shooting with some birds hanging from his belt. He seemed much pleased, and said, 'Look here sir, what a curious bird!' holding out what at first completely puzzled me. I saw a bird with a mass of splendid green feathers on its breast, elongated into two glittering tufts; but what I could not understand was a pair of long white feathers, which stuck straight out from each shoulder. Ali assured me that the bird stuck them out this way itself when fluttering its wings, and that they had remained so without his touching them. I now saw that I had got great prize, no less than a completely new form of bird of paradise, differing most remarkably from every other known bird.

When a specimen of the bird reached the British Museum, it was named *Semioptera wallacei* or 'Wallace's Standard-Wing' in his honour and his name would forever be associated with a new species of one of the most spectacular birds in the world. What is most significant is that this is the only Bird of Paradise to come from Maluku, as all the others come from Aru, Wagio, Papua-New Guinea or Northern Australia. Wallace's Standard-Wing proved to be so rare that in the following century, the bird was only seen once again.

Wallace also describes seeing on Bacan the small flying opossum, which is quite like a small flying squirrel in appearance but is a marsupial. Marsupials, in the form of the *cuscus* or possum, were common throughout the Moluccan islands and were first described by the Portuguese when they arrived in Ambon and Ternate in the 1500s.

Wallace's last and most difficult voyage to Papua was in a small prahu which he had built in Goram (the Gorong Islands southeast of Ceram) and fitted out to accommodate six men, including four crew, an Ambonese hunter and himself. His faithful assistant Ali had recently married in Ternate, and it appears that he had chosen not to join Wallace on this expedition. From Goram, Wallace sailed to the north coast of Ceram, where, for whatever reason, his crew deserted him. After hiring a new crew, they sailed north with much difficulty against the prevailing winds and currents towards the island of Waigio in Papua. Here he stayed for two months and collected some twenty-four specimens of the rare Red Bird of Paradise, which, according to Wallace, only inhabits this island and nowhere else.

Le Paradis rouge n.º 6

> I began to think that we were not to get this magnificent species At length the fruit ripened on the fig tree close to my house and many birds came to feed on it; and one morning as I was taking my coffee a male paradise bird was seen to settle on its top ... the head back and shoulders are clothed with a rich yellow, the deep metallic green colour of the throat extends farther over the head, and the feathers are elongated on the forehead into two little erectile crests. The side-plumes are shorter, but are of a rich red colour, terminating in delicate white points, and the middle tail feathers are represented by two long rigid glossy ribbands, which are black, thin, semi-cylindrical and droop gracefully into a spiral curve.

His accommodation on Waigio was in a small hut which he describes as a 'dwarf's house', just eight feet square and raised on posts so that it was four and a half feet off the ground. He used the space under the hut as his work area, which required the six foot Wallace to enter by bending double and then, with his head just below the floor above him, sit for hours at a small table preparing his specimens.

His return voyage from Waigio to Ternate was again beset by problems. They had great difficulty rounding the southern point of Halmahera while trying to sail against the prevailing winds and currents. In the process, they lost their anchor, nearly ran out of food, and fortunately, were out in deeper water when struck by a tsunami wave. They then encountered a squall so severe that it shredded their tattered sail and his helmsman was forced to stand up and beseech Allah's mercy to help save them. In summary, Wallace describes the voyage to Wagio as the most difficult of his sea voyages and writes:

> My first crew ran away; two men were lost for a month on a desert island; we were ten times aground on coral reefs; the small boat was lost astern; we were thirty-eight days on the voyage home, which should have taken twelve; we were many times

short of food and water; we had no compass lamp, owing to there not being a drop of oil in Waigio when we left; and to crown it all, during the whole of our voyages ... occupying in all seventy-eight days ... we had not one single day of fair wind! We were always close braced up, always struggling against wind, tide, and leeway, and in a vessel that would scarcely sail more than eight points from the wind. Every seaman will admit that my first voyage in my own boat was a most unlucky one.

17

Charles Darwin – On the Origin of Species

Charles Darwin was a cautious man burdened with a bold idea, his big, dangerous idea. In April 1856, Charles Lyell spent a few days at Down House, and it was during this stay that Darwin revealed the theory he had been quietly developing over the last twenty years - his theory of natural selection. Lyell was sceptical but urged Darwin to publish so as to establish priority. Darwin then consulted his friend Joseph Hooker, who had read Darwin's 1844 'Essay' and was already familiar with his thinking. His advice was to wait, to wait until his theory was indisputable.

In July 1858, Wallace's 'Letter from Ternate' reached Darwin at Down House. His reaction was a mixture of amazement and despair, which he described as almost paralysing. In just 4000 words, Wallace had summarised the key elements of the theory of evolution, which Darwin had been labouring over for years. 'I never saw a more striking coincidence, if Wallace had my manuscript sketch written out in 1842, he could not have made a better short abstract'. In this short manuscript, Wallace had summarised all the main principles of Darwin's ideas on species, his work of more than twenty years since returning from the voyage of the *Beagle*. Once Wallace's paper was published, it would have precedence over all of Darwin's years of work, because of his decision not to publish his big, dangerous idea.

Wallace wrote that he hoped his idea would be new to Darwin, and if he thought it sufficiently important, to show it to Sir Charles Lyell. There has been some controversy about exactly when Darwin received Wallace's letter and how quickly he passed it on to Lyell, with the implication that Darwin may have decided to include some of Wallace's ideas in his 1844 Essay. But of course, Joseph Hooker had already seen a copy of this document, so this is highly unlikely.

Darwin had acquired a narrow strip of land of 1.5 acres (0.61 ha) adjoining the grounds of Down House to the southwest and named it Sandwalk Wood. One side was shaded with oak trees, and the other looked over a hedge to a charming valley. Darwin had a variety of trees planted and ordered a path known as the 'sandwalk' to be built around the perimeter. Darwin's daily walk of several circuits of this path served both for exercise and for uninterrupted thinking. His analogy of the tangled meadowbank to describe the web of life and consequently of his concept of Natural Selection would have come from one of his walks around the 'sandwalk' or in the surrounding countryside.

If there were any delays in Darwin forwarding the 'Letter from Ternate' on to Sir Charles Lyell, it may have been because Darwin spent many hours pacing around the 'sandwalk' bordering his property. It was known as his 'thinking path', where on his daily walks Darwin did his most serious thinking, sometimes stopping to gaze at a plant or flower for minutes at a time while contemplating the question that was on his mind. The question on his mind now was, did he want to have the honour that came with the precedence of publication of his big, bad, dangerous idea? Yet this was impossible, as it had remained locked in his desk drawer. He desired the honour of the precedence of publication, but his comfortable life at Down House would never be the same again. He desired the honour of precedence of publication, but would the expected controversy plunge him deeper into his chronic ill-health? He could remain silent and let the relatively unknown Wallace publish the theory. Wallace was never part of the Establishment, probably cared little for it, so why not let him commit what Darwin himself had described as 'a murder' - the murder of the God of Creation! Then, when things settled down, Darwin could publish his full treatise on the subject. Whatever Darwin would decide, he had an obligation to forward Wallace's paper on to Lyell, and his cover letter reads:

> Some years ago, you recommended me to read a paper by Wallace in the 'Annals', which had interested you and as I was writing to him, I knew this would please him much, so I told him. He has today sent me the enclosed and asked me to forward it to you. It seems to me well worth reading. Your words have come true with a vengeance that I should be forestalled ... I have never seen a more striking coincidence, if Wallace had my manuscript Sketch written out in 1842, he could not have made a better short abstract! Even his terms now stand as Heads of my Chapters. Please return me his manuscript which he does not say he wishes me to publish; but I shall of course at once write and offer to send to any Journal. So all my originality, whatever it may amount to, will be smashed. Though my Book, if it will ever have any value, will not be deteriorated; as all the labour consists in the application of the theory.
>
> I hope you will approve of Wallace's sketch, so that I may tell him what you say.

Letters then passed between Lyell, Hooker and Darwin is said to have distanced himself from any decision. A year earlier, in 1857, Darwin had written a letter to an American colleague, Asa Gray, the leading American botanist of the day, asking him to maintain secrecy while summarising his current thoughts on the origin of species, which reads:

The varying offspring of each species will try (only a few will succeed) to seize on as many and as diverse places in the economy of nature as possible. Each new variety or species when formed will generally take the place of and so exterminate its less well-fitted parent. This I believe to be the original of the classification or arrangement of all organic beings at all times. These always seem to branch and sub-branch like a tree from a common trunk; the flourishing twigs destroying the less vigorous; the dead and lost branches rudely representing extinct genera and families.

The date of this letter was documentary proof of his precedence over Wallace's paper, and after more pacing around the 'sandwalk' and more periods of anguished contemplation, Darwin decided that he wanted an outcome that was in his favour and wrote another letter to Lyell:

There is nothing in Wallace's sketch which is not written out much fuller in my Essay copied in 1844 and read by Hooker some dozen years ago. About a year ago, I sent a short sketch of my views to Asa Grey, so that I can truly say and prove that I take nothing from Wallace. I should be extremely glad now to publish a sketch of my general views in about a dozen pages or so. But I cannot persuade myself that I can do so honourably. Wallace says nothing about publication, and I enclose his letter. – But as I had not intended to publish any sketch, can I do so honourably because Wallace has sent me an outline of his doctrine? – I would rather burn my whole book, than that he or any other man should think that I have behaved in such a paltry spirit. Do you think that his having sent me this sketch ties my hands?

Lyell and Hooker worked on reaching a compromise, which they thought would be fair to both parties. They would arrange a joint publication of Darwin's 1844 essay, together with Wallace's paper, at a special meeting of the Linnean Society to be held at the beginning of July 1858. Darwin would not be present at the meeting, as tragically, he was burying his little boy on the same day. Hooker and Lyell were present and introduced the papers in order of writing. That is, Darwin's unpublished 1844 Essay, which he sent to Hooker, his 1857 letter to Asa Grey the American naturalist, and then Wallace's 1858 Ternate paper *On the Tendency of Varieties to Depart Indefinitely from the Original Type*. At that time, Wallace was somewhere in the wilds of Papua and could not be consulted on the presentation of his paper, but by presenting the documents in the order of writing, Darwin was given scientific precedence. Lyell and Hooker both signed the letter which introduced the papers, which, as was customary, were read by the Secretary:

> My Dear Sir,
> The accompanying papers, which we have the honour of communicating to the Linnean Society, and which all relate to the same subject, viz. the Laws which affect the Production of Varieties, Races, and Species, contain the results of the investigations of two indefatigable naturalists, Mr Charles Darwin and Mr Alfred Wallace.
> These gentlemen having, independently and unknown to one another, conceived the same very ingenious theory to account for the appearance and perpetuation of varieties and of specific forms on our planet, may both fairly claim the merit of being original thinkers in this important line of enquiry; but neither of them having published his views, though Mr Darwin has for many years past been repeatedly urged to do so, and both authors having now unreservedly placed their papers in our hands, we think it would best promote the interests of sci-

ence that a selection from them should be laid before the Linnean Society.

Charles Lyell

Jos. D. Hooker

Proceedings of the Linnean Society, 1858

Joseph Hooker describes the meeting and the response after the presentation of the papers:

> The interest excited was intense, but the subject too novel and too ominous for the old school to enter the lists, before armouring. After the meeting it was talked over with bated breath: Lyell's approval, and perhaps in a small way mine, as his lieutenant in the affair, rather overawed the Fellows, who would otherwise have flown out against the doctrine.

At the end of that year Thomas Bell, the President of the Linnean Society and himself obviously opposed to Darwin's theory, declared in his annual presidential address to the Society that "The past year has not, indeed, been marked by any of those striking discoveries which at once revolutionise, so to speak, the department of science in which they occur".

After his return from his voyages to Papua and when the mail eventually reached Ternate, Wallace was excited to find letters from both Charles Darwin and Joseph Hooker explaining the procedure of the joint presentation to the Linnean Society and hoping he would approve. From his relatively solitary existence in a remote and obscure location on the other side of the world, and having just had a number of near-death experiences while on his voyage to Wagio and return to Ternate, this seemed like a miracle. Not knowing all the details of what had happened, Wallace wrote excitedly to his mother:

I sent Mr Darwin an essay on a subject upon which he is now writing a great work. He showed it to Dr Hooker and Sir Charles Lyell, who thought so highly of it that they had it read before the Linnean Society. This ensures me the acquaintance of these eminent men on my return home.

Wallace then wrote a response to Darwin's letter, and he received this reply in which Darwin explains that he has now given up on completing the large work or magnum opus representing his twenty years of studies:

My Dear Sir,

I was extremely much pleased at receiving three days ago your letter to me and that to Dr. Hooker. Permit me to say how heartily I admire the spirit in which they are written. Though I had absolutely nothing whatever to do in leading Lyell and Hooker to what they thought a fair course of action, yet I naturally could not but feel anxious to hear what your impression would be. I owe indirectly much to you and them; for I almost think that Lyell would have proved right and I should never have completed my larger work … My abstract will make a small volume of 400 hundred or 500 pages. Whenever published, I will of course send you a copy.

Darwin wanted to get into print as soon as possible, and in twelve months, he completed his smaller volume and rushed it to the printer. *On the Origin of Species* or in its full title *On the Origin of Species by Means of Natural Selection, or the Preservation of Favoured Races in the Struggle for Life* was published in November 1859. It sold out on the first day of publication and has never been out of print since. His theory is simply stated in the introduction:

As many more individuals of each species are born than can possibly survive; and as, consequently, there is a frequently recurring struggle for existence, it follows that any being, if it vary however slightly in any manner profitable to itself, under the complex and sometimes varying conditions of life, will have a better chance of surviving, and thus be *naturally selected*. From the strong principle of inheritance, any selected variety will tend to propagate its new and modified form.

In his book, he acknowledged Wallace's field work, but Darwin's name was forever linked with the theory of evolution by natural selection. Darwin was careful to point out that he had come to the decision to publish his ideas over a long period of time, as his introduction to *On the Origin of Species* reads:

When on board HMS *Beagle*, as a naturalist, I was much struck with certain facts in the distribution of the inhabitants of South America, and in the geological relations of the present to the past inhabitants of that continent. These facts seemed to throw some light on the origin of species – that mystery of mysteries, as it has been called by one of our greatest philosophers. On my return home, it occurred to me, in 1837 that something might be made out on this question by patiently accumulating and reflecting on all sorts of facts which could possibly have a bearing on it. After five years work, I allowed myself to speculate on the subject and drew up some short notes; these I enlarged in 1844 into an Essay of the conclusions which then seemed probable; from that period to the present day I have steadily pursued the same object. I hope that I may be excused for entering these personal details, as I give them to show that I have not been hasty in coming to a decision.

On the Origin of Species destroyed at one blow the recent tradition of the Church of England, which was Natural Theology. All the beautiful and ingenious contrivances in nature, which Natural Theology explained as the benevolent design of the Creator, could now be explained by the operation of natural selection. Although he was careful not to mention it, Darwin's theory meant that humans were part of the same tree of life as all other organisms. The idea of 'survival of the fittest' as the mechanism for the evolution of species now seems so obvious and simple. Why had nobody thought of it before? But to the Church and general population of the day, it was unthinkable since they believed that all creatures were created by God in their present form and that species were fixed.

As Darwin had anticipated and what may have caused his considerable ill health for many years was the hostile reaction from the Church and the Establishment. The first problem was that Natural Selection left no place for Divine Purpose or Divine Intervention. The second problem was that even though Darwin had studiously avoided the subject, in the end the debate always came around to the relationship between man and ape. His 'Theory' was decried in the grand Cathedrals and the village churches across Britain. The treatise 'The Darwinian Theory Examined', by Bickers and Son, takes this criticism to the extreme:

> Vast numbers of virtuous vestrymen frighten the old women of their parishes with the mere mention of his name ... his conspiracy against the peace of the British matron is so diabolical that even the Bishop's thunder against him, and a good number of people of an old fashioned way of thinking have a conviction that he ought to be burned either in this world, or another.

Darwin sent a copy of *On the Origin of Species* to Robert FitzRoy in recognition of the opportunity granted him by being chosen to sail with him on the *Beagle*. Over the years, and certainly after his marriage, FitzRoy had become even more fundamentalist in his religious beliefs, and the idea that he had provided the vehicle for Darwin's theory was a complete anathema to him. He hated the book and wrote back, 'My dear old friend, I, at least, cannot find anything ennobling in the thought of being a descendant of even the most ancient Ape' and he seized upon every opportunity to denounce *The Origin* and its author.

In Rome, Darwin was accused of heresy. Pope Pius IX placed the book on the 'Index Expurgatorius', which meant that no Catholic could read it. In Britain, Cardinal Manning organised a society to fight this new, 'so-called science, which declares there is no God and that Adam was an ape'. The Bishop of Oxford charged that 'the concept of natural selection attempts to limit the power of God, the Bible and dishonours nature - was Darwin proposing that Queen Victoria was related to an ape?' Darwin's former geology mentor at Cambridge, the Rev. Adam Sedgwick, wrote a scathing review that appeared in the *Spectator* in which he expressed his detestation of the theory, and wrote to Darwin:

> I read your book with more pain than pleasure. Parts of it I admired greatly; parts of it I laughed until my sides were almost sore, other parts I read with absolute sorrow, because I think them utterly false and mischievous - you have deserted – after a start in that tram-road of solid physical truth – the true path of induction ... There is a moral or metaphysical part of nature as well as a physical. A man who denies this is deep in the mire of folly.

However, there were those willing to give him support, including the biologist and Gold Medallist of the Royal Society, Thomas Huxley, who described himself as being bowled over by *The Origin*:

> My Dear Darwin,
>
> Since I read Von Bar's essays, nine years ago, no work on Natural History Science I have met with has made so great an impression on me ... I trust you will not allow yourself to be in any way disgusted or annoyed by the considerable abuse and misrepresentation which, unless I greatly mistake, is in store for you. Depend upon it you have earned the lasting gratitude of all thoughtful men. And as to the curs which will bark and yelp, you must recollect that some of your friends, at any rate, are endowed with an amount of combativeness which (though you have often and justly rebuked it) may stand in your good stead.

Huxley became one of Darwin's staunchest defenders. A fiery supporter of Darwin's ideas, he assumed the role of Darwin's champion and by facing down his detractors and promoting his theories, he soon became known as 'Darwin's Bulldog'. A few months after the publication of *The Origin,* there was a public showdown in Oxford between Bishop Samuel Wilberforce and Thomas Huxley at a meeting of the British Association for the Advancement of Science. This was the same Samuel Wilberforce who, while a parish Reverend, had advised the local squires to take education in hand lest the country folk learn "a smattering of science" and forget their God-given duties. Bishop Wilberforce began the dialogue by boldly stating:

> "Has any one such instance of natural selection ever been discovered? We fearlessly assert not one!" He then baited Huxley by asking him, "If he was related to an ape on his grandmother's or grandfather's side". In response, Huxley answered that "I would rather have a miserable ape for a grandfather than a man possessed of great means and influence who employs that influence for the mere purpose of introducing ridicule into a serious scientific discussion – I unhesitatingly affirm my preference for the ape".

Or as the popular press described it, Huxley responded by saying, 'I would rather be an ape than a Bishop.' The meeting descended into chaos, and the scientists began arguing amongst themselves. In the centre of the room, his face contorted with rage, Robert FitzRoy could be seen waving a Bible over his head while denouncing Darwin and all his works.

In April 1860 the *Edinburgh Review* published Richard Owen's anonymous review of *The Origin*. In it, Owen showed his anger at what he saw as Darwin's caricature of the creationist position and for ignoring his own theory, 'Of the continuous operation of the ordained becoming of living things'. He also attacked Darwin's 'disciples', Hooker and Huxley, for their 'short-sighted adherence'. Darwin thought his review 'spiteful, extremely malignant, clever, and... damaging' and later commented that "The Londoners say he is mad with envy because my book is so talked about. It is painful to be hated in the intense degree with which Owen hates me."

Wallace received his copy of *The Origin* while in Ambon on his way to Ceram and then Wagio. He wrote to Charles Darwin expressing his admiration for the book, and this time Darwin replied by addressing him personally:

> My Dear Wallace,
> I received this morning your letter from Ambon containing some remarks and you high approbation of my book. Your letter has pleased me very much, and I most completely agree with you on the parts which are strongest and which are weakest ... before telling you about progress of opinion on the subject, you must let me say how I admire the generous manner in which you speak of my Book: most persons would in your position have felt some jealousy. How nobly free you seem to be of this common failing of mankind. But you speak far too modestly of

yourself; you would, if you had my leisure done the work just as well, perhaps better, than I have done it.

Caricature of Darwin as an Ape
The Hornet, **1871**

Talking of envy, you never read anything more envious and spiteful than Owen is in the Edinburgh Review ... The attacks have been heavy and incessant of late. Sedgwick and Professor Clark attacked me savagely at the Cambridge Philosophical Society, but Henslow defended me well although not a convert. Phillips has since attacked me in a lecture at Cambridge. Sir W. Jardine in the New Philosophical Journal. Wollaston in the Annals of Natural History. A. Murray before the Royal Society of Edinburgh. Houghton at the Geological Society of Dublin. Dawson in the Canadian Naturalist Magazine, and many others. But I am got case-hardened and all these attacks will make me only more determined to fight.

Case-hardened? His dilemma of whether to publish *On the Origin of Species* had been decided. His big, dangerous idea was now public, and the ensuing controversy seemed to have revived the Darwin of his youth. The Charles Darwin who had spent months riding the Argentinian pampas with the gauchos, sleeping rough, and consorting with generals and revolutionaries. There were challenges to be met and the elderly and perennially ill Darwin was for now, at least, cast aside. The newly invigorated Charles Darwin and his lieutenants, Joseph Hooker and Thomas Huxley were ready to go into battle for an idea whose time had come.

18

Alfred Russel Wallace – The Return to England

Wallace received his copy of *On the Origin of Species* from the monthly Dutch mail steamer while he was in Ambon. According to his notes, he read and re-read the book five or six times with increasing admiration for its vast accumulation of evidence and its overwhelming argument for the evolution of species. There was no hint of rancour or jealousy when he wrote:

> The cycles of astronomy or even the periods of geology will alone enable us to appreciate the vast depths of time we have to contemplate in the endeavour to understand the slow growth of life upon the earth … Mr Darwin has given the world a new science, and his name should in my opinion, stand above that of every philosopher of ancient or modern times. The force of admiration can no further go!!

In fact, Wallace may have felt relieved that he would not have to experience the personal attacks that were now being directed against Charles Darwin. At least Darwin had the prestige and determined backing of his friends and fellow scientists like Lyell, Hooker and

Huxley, which the relatively unknown Wallace may not have received. Now thirty-nine years old, Wallace was ready to return to England. A particularly long and dangerous voyage back to Ternate from the island of Wagio had used up all his energy, and he was prepared to admit in letters home that 'My health, too, gives way and I cannot now put up so well with fatigue and privations as at first'.

Notwithstanding his fatigue, he took a circuitous route home while trying to fill in the gaps in his knowledge of the archipelago. He followed the route of the monthly Dutch mail steamer, stopping first at the islands of Timor and Buru, then returning back to Ternate, before stopping in Manado, Macassar, Surabaya, Batavia and finally in South Sumatra on his way to Singapore. In Singapore, Wallace parted with his faithful and reliable Ali. It was Ali who had accompanied him during his travels around Indonesia, who had learned to shoot and skin birds, who had cooked for him, and nursed him back to health during his various illnesses. He also became a reliable boatman, and in several instances, he could have helped save both their lives. Wallace took him to a photographic studio and had a portrait taken of Ali in European clothes:

> On parting, besides a present in money. I gave him my two double-barreled guns and whatever ammunition I had, with a lot of surplus stores ... which made him quite rich. Here he adopted European clothes, which did not suit him nearly so well as his native dress, and thus, clad, a friend took a very good photograph of him. I therefore now present his likeness to my readers as that of the best native servant I ever had, and the faithful companion of almost all my journeying's among the islands of the Far East.

Photo of Ali taken in Singapore, 1862

Ali had met a girl and married while they were in Ternate and he returned to her there. Forty years later the American naturalist Thomas Barbour describes visiting Ternate and meeting a man who introduced himself as 'Ali Wallace'. He was now already an old man but reminisced of the times he spent in the jungles with Wallace and of nursing him back to health after an infected wound or an attack of malaria.

In Singapore Wallace packed up his remaining specimens and after his Brazil experience he took the precaution of sending them in different boats sailing for England. Wallace himself sailed from Singapore in 1862 with two prized possessions in his luggage. He had acquired two Lesser Birds of Paradise. These beauties of the natural world would be dazzling examples of his years spent in the archipelago and his voyages to its most eastern extremities in Maluku and Papua. They would be the first live Birds of Paradise to reach England in many years and he nurtured them with great care on the voyage back to England:

> On my way home, I stayed a week at Bombay, to break the journey, and to lay in a fresh stock of bananas for my birds. I had great difficulty, however, in supplying them with insect food, for in the Peninsular and Orient steamers, cockroaches were scarce, and it was only by setting traps in the store rooms, and by hunting every night in the forecastle, that I could secure

a few dozen of these creatures – scarcely enough for a single meal.

His arrival back in England was anticipated by *The Times* who published an article that after an eight year absence, Mr A. R. Wallace, the well-known traveller and naturalist, was returning to London with his two live Birds of Paradise.

Back in London, Wallace found himself surrounded by packing-cases containing all the specimens he had sent home for his private collection. The most important specimens needed to be described and some of the more interesting problems of variation and geographical distribution be studied:

Wallace in Singapore before departing for England, 1862

> When I reached England in the spring of 1862. I found myself surrounded by a room full of packing cases, containing the collections that I had from time to time sent home for my private use. These comprised nearly three thousand bird skins, of about a thousand species, and at least twenty thousand beetles and butterflies, of about seven thousand species, besides some quadrupeds and land shells. A large proportion of these I had not seen for years, and in my then weak state of health, the unpacking, sorting, and arranging of such a mass of specimens occupied a long time.

After he recovered his health, Wallace accepted Darwin's invitation to visit him at Down House. They enjoyed each other's company and conversed either in Darwin's study or as they paced around the 'sandwalk'. Wallace liked the family atmosphere at Down House. This was a life he could contemplate for himself once he had settled down and found a wife. Their mutual affection was genuine, and the relationship continued through their correspondence and the occasional lunch when Darwin came up to London. Although they were now equals, Wallace's roots went deep into the social structure of Victorian England, and he always saw Darwin as his social and scientific superior.

The first mark of his recognition in London was election as a Fellow of the Zoological Society. In the succeeding years, he published eighteen papers in the Transactions or Proceedings of the Linnean Society. In June 1863, he read one of his most important papers before the Royal Geographical Society, entitled *On the Physical Geography of the Malay Archipelago*.

His friend Henry Walter Bates had returned from Brazil in 1859 and was encouraged by Charles Darwin to write up his eleven-year stay on the Amazon. His book entitled *The Naturalist on the River Amazons - A Record of the Adventures, Habits of Animals, Sketches of Brazilian and Indian Life, and Aspects of Nature under the Equator, during Eleven*

Years of Travel was published in 1863. Bates's account of his stay, including observations of nature and the people around him, occupies most of this book. The result was widely admired, although some reviewers disagreed with the book's support for Darwin's theory of evolution, but they generally enjoyed his account of the journey, scenery, people and natural history. His main scientific contribution was his observations of the colouration of butterflies, which led him to describe what is now called Batesian mimicry, where an edible species protects itself by appearing like a distasteful species. Bates observed how they fly in the same parts of the forest as their model and are often in company with them. So a scarce, edible species takes on the appearance of an abundant, noxious species. Predators, Bates supposed, learn to avoid the noxious species, and a degree of protection covers the edible species. Darwin was particularly struck by Bates's evidence of mimicry, especially in the butterflies of the genus *Heliconius*, for here was some evidence of speciation actually in progress, and he wrote:

> The facts just given are therefore of some scientific importance, for they tend to show that a physiological species can be and is produced in nature out of the varieties of a pre-existing closely allied one. This is not an isolated case… But in very few has it happened that the species which clearly appears to be the parent, co-exists with one that has been evidently derived from it.

Darwin wrote to Bates describing it as 'the best book of Natural History' and was delighted with his support of evolution. Darwin thought that the conservative magazine *Athenaeum* had reviewed the book 'coldly and insolently' and in his own appreciation for the *Natural History Review*, he references Bates's lack of reading material in the Amazon jungle and produces some subtle wit that shows a sense of humour that Darwin may have had in person, but is rarely seen in his writing:

> Mr. Bates must indeed have been driven to great straits as regards his mental food, when, as he tells us, he took to reading the *Athenaeum* three times over, "the first time devouring the more interesting articles—the second, the whole of the remainder—and the third, reading all the advertisements from beginning to end.

When Wallace finally completed his scientific work, and after writing thirty papers for publication in various scientific journals, he then had time to start thinking about a book of his travels in the Far East, and he wrote to Charles Darwin in January 1864:

> I am at last making a beginning of a small book on my Eastern Journey, which, if I can persevere, I hope to have ready by Christmas. I am a very bad hand at writing anything like narrative. I want something to argue on, and then I find it much easier to go ahead. I rather despair, therefore, of making so good a book as Bates' though I think my subject is better.

In the spring of 1865, Wallace made contact with the Mitten family who lived in the Sussex village of Hurstpierpoint, where he delighted to see the wildflowers growing in the woods around their house and enjoyed botanising with their eldest daughter, Annie. As he described in his autobiography, 'This similarity of taste led to a close intimacy, and in the spring of the following year I was married to Mr Mitten's eldest daughter, then about eighteen years old.' In June 1867, Annie gave birth to a boy who was christened Herbert Spencer Wallace in memory of Wallace's younger brother. They returned from London to live in Hurtspierpoint, where Annie's family could help with the baby and Wallace could benefit from the isolation to work on his travel book. In 1868, Wallace's contribution to science was recognised by the award of the Royal Medal by the Royal Society, which was an important acknowledgement of his scientific contributions, and in January 1869, his daughter Violet was born.

The Malay Archipelago was published in March 1869. Fortunately, the reviews and sales were positive, which provided Wallace with some steady income for the first time since his return to England. In the preface, Wallace explains why he delayed writing his book for six years after his return, saying that waiting for the results of the study of his collections has given the reader a much more interesting and instructive book. Based on the four field journals he kept during his eight years in Malaysia and Indonesia, it is still the greatest travel book on the region. After receiving his copy of *The Malay Archipelago* Darwin wrote:

> I was delighted at receiving your book this morning. The whole appearance and the illustrations with which it is so profusely ornamented are quite beautiful ... That you have returned alive is wonderful after all your risk from illness and sea voyages, especially the most interesting one to Waigeo and back. Of all the impressions which I have received from your book, the strongest is that your perseverance in the cause of science was heroic.

It is remarkable that nowhere in *The Malay Archipelago* does Wallace refer to his discovery of the origin of species or his paper *On the Tendency of Varieties to Depart Indefinitely from the Original Type*. He gives all the honour to Charles Darwin as the Frontispiece to the book reads:

To Charles Darwin
Author of 'The Origin of Species'
I dedicate this work
Not only
As a token of my personal esteem and friendship
but also
to express my deep admiration
for
his genius and his works

Charles Darwin's personal copy of *The Malay Archipelago,* British Museum

The first edition of *The Malay Archipelago,* 1500 copies in two volumes, quickly sold out, and a second edition of 750 copies also sold out. Translations were made into German and Dutch, and his book has never been out of print. It is a wonderful book and apart from being both a travel journal and scientific work, *The Malay Archipelago* is written with simplicity, clarity and the most remarkable literary elegance, as can be seen in this example from his time in Macassar:

It was the beginning of December, and the rainy season at Macassar had just set in. For nearly three months I had beheld the sun rise daily above the palm groves, mount to the zenith, and descend like a globe of fire into the ocean, unobscured for a single moment of its course. Now dark leaden clouds had gathered over the whole heavens, and it seemed to have rendered him permanently invisible. The strong east winds, warm and dry and dust-laden, which had hitherto blown as certainly as the sun had risen, were now replaced by variable gusty breezes and heavy rains, often continuous for three days and nights together; and the parched and fissured rice stubbles, which during the dry weather had extended in every direction for miles around the town, were already so flooded as to be only passable by boats, or by means of a labyrinth of paths on top of the narrow banks which divided the separate properties.

During his time in the jungles of the Indonesian archipelago, Wallace would have dreamed of returning to England and living in a grand country home as a 'gentleman scientist'. He loved searching for the ideal country location and then designing and building his own home. Unfortunately, the cost of these ventures usually exceeded his income and after occupying them for a few years he would be forced to sell and move his family somewhere else. Wallace continued to look for a suitable country home, and he found a four acre site near the River Thames and the village of Grays about twenty miles east of London. He was himself involved in building the house and the family moved in in March 1872, three months after the birth of his son William and a few weeks after he was elected a Fellow of the Linnean Society. He finally settled in a house at Broadstone in Dorset, which he purchased in 1890 because 'of the rich golden clumps of the dwarf gorse and because rhododendrons and water-lilies could be grown in the garden'.

Wallace seemed to have inherited some of his father's characteristic incaution with money, and after supporting his extended family and making some poor investments, he was never financially independent. Finally, through the efforts of Darwin, Huxley and Hooker, he was awarded in 1881 a government pension which provided a steady income for the rest of his life. It had been a long campaign to gain this recognition, but Darwin's persistence on his behalf had finally paid off.

At the age of fifty, Alfred Russel Wallace had for the first time in his life a regular income, and his thanks to Charles Darwin were heartfelt:

> I must again return to you my best thanks, and assure you that there is no one living to whose kindness in such a matter I could feel myself indebted with so much pleasure and satisfaction.

Epilogue

The Wallace Line still stands as the western-most reach of Australian species, but there are now additional lines. The Weber Line is the eastern-most extent of Asian species and these two lines surround the enigmatic island of Sulawesi. The Lydeckker Line follows close to the Australian continental shelf and is the westernmost extent of Australian mammals.

On the Origin of Species received a devastating review by a Scottish engineer named Fleeming Jenkin. In his review, Jenkin pointed out that Darwin's theory foundered because there was no possibility of a new variant spreading throughout a population. The prevalent theory of inheritance was that of blending and that offspring were a blend of their parents' characteristics. Therefore, any useful new variation should begin to be blended out as soon as the animal or plant starts breeding with the 'normal' population.

Darwin knew this was a weakness and his incomplete research was another reason for delaying his publication. He needed a mechanism of inheritance that could account for the reproduction, generation after generation, of a stable, inheritable variation on which natural selection could work. How was an advantageous trait passed on, and more importantly, how did it persist? In an attempt to solve this question, he bred snapdragons, crossing those bearing red flowers with those bearing white flowers. He gathered information from plant and animal breeders. He joined a pigeon fanciers club and experimented with breeding pigeons himself. What was the mechanism by which cross-breeding worked? To get an insider's view of this craft, he joined different pigeon clubs, both high and low, and met with more of the human species than was his norm. 'I am hand and glove with all sorts of Fanciers, Spitalfield weavers and all sorts of odd specimens of the Human species, who fancy Pigeons'.

Darwin published a paper entitled *Variations of Animals and Plants Under Domestication* in which he proposed a theory of inheritance which he called pangenesis, where cells and tissues in the body adapt to the environment and these cells are shed into the blood-stream as 'gemmules', which eventually lodge in the sex organs and are then passed on to the next generation. He had no experimental evidence for this, but he needed a unit of inheritance transmitted through sexual reproduction. But this still did not answer the question of 'blending' and the continuation of inheritance for generation after generation.

The answer to this question lay with an obscure friar living in a Monastery in Brno, Czechoslovakia, who became particularly interested in plant breeding. On October 9, 1843, Gregor Mendel was admitted to the convent of the Augustinians as a novice. He was familiar with the works of both Darwin and Wallace and a well-marked copy of *On the Origin of Species* was found in his library. He spent eight years from 1856 until 1863 counting the different kinds of offspring from crossing pea plants, which bore either wrinkled or smooth seeds. He followed them through second and third generations and published his results in 1865. Scientists at the time believed that inherited characteristics were blended in the offspring, which meant that a selective advantage needed for natural selection would be 'blended out' in a few generations. What Mendel's experiments showed is that characteristics inherited from each parent were not lost in a mixing process, but remained in discrete parcels (or genes) which could then be passed on to later generations. His findings were published as a forty-four page article in the Proceedings of the Scientific Society of Bron in 1865 and were then virtually ignored for the rest of Mendel's life.

Mendel's painstaking research led to the result Darwin was looking for, and if only he had known of his work, then Darwin's argument for the evolution of species would have been completely convincing. Amazingly, this knowledge lay in Darwin's study, for after his death, a copy of an 1881 book by Focke called *Plant Hybridization*, which cited Mendel's work, was found in his library with the bound pages still uncut and therefore unread. It was in 1918 that Ronald Fisher, an English statistician, combined Mendelian genetics with the theory of Natural Selection and, in 1930, published a book called *The Genetical Theory of Natural Selection*, which gave Natural Selection a mathematical footing and broad scientific consensus.

Darwin died at the age of 74, and his funeral took place at Westminster Abbey on Wednesday, 26 April 1882. Darwin himself had wished for a simple burial at his local church, close to Down House and next to the burial place of his beloved children who had died in their infancy. For most of his life, Darwin was only a nominal Christian, and he later described himself as an agnostic after the invention of that word by Thomas Huxley. Many of his disciples, including Huxley, campaigned relentlessly for the high honour of a burial at Westminster Abbey. Huxley argued that "In 50 or a 100 years hence it would seem incredible to people that the State did not recognise his transcendent services to science". Darwin had become Britain's most prominent scientist and countries like France and Germany had awarded him their highest honours.

For many, it was unthinkable that Darwin be buried in Westminster Abbey. Had not the Church of England only twenty years earlier described Darwin as 'The Devil's Disciple'? Yet two thousand mourners representing a cross-section of the Victorian Establishment attended Westminster Abbey for his funeral. Except that is, for a few notable absences – Queen Victoria was busy preparing for her son's wedding, Prime Minister Gladstone had the Irish problem to contend with, the Archbishop of Canterbury was unfortunately indisposed, and the Dean of Westminster Abbey happened to be abroad.

Ten pallbearers carried his coffin from the Church, including two Dukes, a Lord, several Ambassadors and his close friends and scientific collaborators - Thomas Huxley, Joseph Hooker and most importantly, the co-discoverer of the origin of species – Alfred Russel Wallace. After the ceremony, one of the Lords apparently asked Huxley, "Do you believe that Darwin was right?" "Of course he was right!" replied Huxley. His lordship then looked around the vastness of the Abbey with a pained expression on his face and said in a low tone, "Couldn't he have just kept it to himself?" Which of course is what he did for twenty years - until the unexpected and probably unwelcome arrival of Alfred Russel Wallace's 'Letter from Ternate'.

The Linnean gold medal awarded to Wallace.

In 1908, the Linnean Society observed the fiftieth anniversary of the 'joint publication' of Darwin's and Wallace's papers by casting a gold medal with the busts of the two great scientists on either side. It was presented to Alfred Russel Wallace as the living co-founder of the theory of natural selection, in the manner of a Nobel Prize of its time. In that same year, Wallace received the Order of Merit from King Edward, which is the highest decoration for achievement given by the Crown for those who have distinguished themselves in science, literature, and the arts.

Despite all his exertions in the Malay and Indonesian Archipelago, Wallace lived to a grand old age of ninety-one and died in 1913. Some of his friends suggested that he be buried in Westminster Abbey, but his wife followed his wishes and had him buried in a small cemetery near his home at Broadstone, Dorset after a service conducted by the Bishop of Salisbury. Later, several prominent British scientists formed a committee to have a medallion of Alfred Russel Wallace placed in Westminster Abbey near where Darwin is buried, which was unveiled on 1 November 1915. A memorial written by E.R. Sykes of the Dorset Field Club reads:

> By the death of Alfred Russel Wallace, the last link with the great workers on evolution, whose names adorn the mid-nineteenth century, is broken. One by one, Darwin, Hooker, Huxley, &c., they have passed away, and now death has taken from us the last, and one of the greatest. We, of the Dorset Field Club, have a special interest in Wallace; he was an Ordinary Member of the Club for some years, and in 1909 became one of our Honorary Members; to many of us he was personally known, and not a mere abstract personality ... Wallace occupied his rightful position as one of the leaders of scientific thought; slowly, but steadily, recognition and honors poured in upon him; and he held his place until death, on November 7th, 1913, in his ninety first year, removed him from amongst us.

The lives and works of Carl Linnaeus, Joseph Banks, Charles Darwin and Alfred Russel Wallace intersect in the collections of the Natural History Museum in South Kensington, London. The Museum has one of the finest collections of Linnean materials in the world, both in terms of size and rarity. With the publication of *Systema Naturae* (1735), Linnaeus introduced a new system for classifying the natural world. Initially, an 11-page pamphlet, the work was expanded by Linnaeus over many years. By the time the 10th edition was published in 1758, it had become a substantial two-volume set. The Linnean Collection at the Museum comprises approximately 12,000 items, with publication dates spanning over 300 years.

The Joseph Banks Collection is officially designated as historic by the Museum's trustees with 4,000 specimens of insects, including beetles, butterflies and moths, and material collected by Banks and Solander during their circumnavigation of the globe on the *Endeavour*. The Joseph Banks Herbarium was originally left to the Linnean Society, but was given to the British Museum by the society in 1863 and subsequently transferred to the Natural History Museum after it first opened in 1881. At that time his statue stood beside a door in an upper gallery that led into the vast Banksian Herbarium. Its massive wooden cabinets containing the dried plants brought back by the *Endeavour* in 1771 and in the adjoining library were huge gilded morocco and calf portfolios containing some of the superb paintings and etchings of the plants collected in Australia which are now part of the historic Banks' *Florilegium* published by the Museum in the 1980s.

In 2006 the Natural History Museum acquired the largest collection of works by and about Charles Darwin in existence. The collection comprises 1,628 works written by Darwin, including 477 versions of *On the Origin of Species* with many in different languages. Although Darwin did not have a formal connection to the Museum, his work underpins all modern research in evolutionary biology, which is a major area of study for scientists at the museum. After Darwin died, the nation honoured the founder of evolutionary theory by putting his marble statue on the landing of the Natural History Museum - his rival Richard Owen's own cathedral. Richard Owen had waged a long and nasty battle against the Darwinian revolution and had to live with this slight until his own death in 1892. Then in 1927, some lingering Owen loyalists managed to get Darwin moved out and Owen moved in. Then, some eighty years later, in May 2009, during the 200th anniversary of Darwin's birth and the 150th anniversary of the publication of *On the Origin of Species,* the museum plucked Robert Owen off his pedestal and put Charles Darwin back in his former place on the landing in the main hall of the Museum.

The Portrait of Alfred Russel Wallace now hanging in The Natural History Museum

The Natural History Museum holds the Wallace Collection of memorabilia, including letters, notebooks, documents, and specimens that he collected on his expeditions to Brazil and the Malay Archipelago. Sometimes described as 'the most famous scientist that you have never heard of' Wallace's contribution to the discovery of evolution seemed to have been almost forgotten by the Natural History Museum, but thanks to the efforts of Bill Bailey, a fervent admirer, Wallace's portrait which for years had been kept in a storeroom at the museum, now hangs in the Main Hall above the statue of the seated Charles Darwin. On the 100th anniversary of his death in November 2013, a statue of Alfred Russel Wallace was unveiled by Sir David Attenborough. Wallace is holding a butterfly net and looking upwards towards a bronze model of a golden birdwing butterfly on the glass façade of the building. The sculpture depicts that defining moment when Wallace sees the magnificent golden birdwing butterfly for the first time in the rainforest of Bacan Island, the same location where he also collected the rare Bird of Paradise, later named *Semioptera wallacei* or 'Wallace's Standard Wing', which he considered his and his assistant Ali's greatest collecting achievement.

Bibliography

Archer, Hand & Godthelp, Australia's Lost World, Reed Books, 1991

Armstrong, Patrick, Darwin's Luck, Continuum UK, 2009

Aughton, Peter, Endeavour, Cassell and Co., 2002

Aydon, Cyril, Charles Darwin, Constable and Robinson, 2002

Banks, Joseph, The Endeavour Journal, Angus and Robertson, 1998

Beaglehole, Joseph Banks Volume 1, Angus and Robertson, 1962

Beaglehole, Joseph Banks Volume 2, Angus and Robertson, 1962

Beld, John van den, Nature of Australia, ABC Books, 1988

Berra, Tim, A Natural History of Australia, UNSW Press, 1998

Berry, Andrew, Infinite Tropics, Verso, 2002

Blair, Lawrence & Lorne, Ring of Fire, Editions Didier Millet, 2010

Bonney, T.G, Charles Lyell and modern geology, Cassell, 1895

Boulter, Michael, Darwin's Garden, Constable and Robinson, 2008

Browne, Janet, Darwin's Origin of Species, Atlantic Books, 2006

Cameron, Hector, Sir Joseph Banks, Angus and Robertson, 1952

Carr, D.J, Sydney Parkinson, Australian National University, 1983

Darwin, Charles, The Voyage of the Beagle, White Star, 2006

Darwin, C, The Origin of Species, Oxford University Press, 1969

Darwin, C, The Beagle Letters, Cambridge University Press, 2008

Darwin, C, An Australian Selection, National Museum of Australia, 2008

Duyker, Edward, Natures Argonaut, The Miegunyah Press,

Duyker, Edward and Tingbrand, Per, Daniel Solander, The Miegunyah Press, 1995

Edgerton & Lochman, Wildlife of Australia, Allen and Unwin, 2009

Fara, P, Sex, Botany & Empire, Columbia University Press, 2004
Flannery, Tim, An Explorer's Notebook, Text Publishing, 2007
Frame, Tom, Evolution in the Antipodes, UNSW Press, 2009
George, Alexander, Banksias, Bloomings Books, 2008
Hall, Robert, Australia - SE Asia Collision, The Geological Society of London, 2011
Hamilton, Jill the Duchess of and Bryce, Julia, The Flower Chain, Kangeroo Press, 1998
Hay, Ashley, Gum, Duffy and Snellgrove, 2002
Hemming, John, Naturalists in Paradise, Thames and Hudson, 2015
Henig, R, A Monk and Two Peas, Weidenfeld & Nicholson, 2000
Johnson, D, The Geology of Australia, Cambridge University Press, 2009
Keynes, Richard, Fossils, Finches & Fuegians, Harper Collins, 2002
Knapp, Sandra, Alfred Russel Wallace in the Amazon, Natural History Museum
Lines, W, Taming the Great South Land, Allen & Unwin, 1991
Low, Tim, Where Song Began, Penguin/Viking, 2014
Mackness, Brian, Prehistoric Australia, Golden Press, 1987
Mawer, Simon, Gregor Mendel, Harry N. Abrams, 2006
McCalman, Iain, Darwin's Armada, Simon and Schuster, 2009
Moorhead, Alan, Darwin and the Beagle, Hamish Hamilton, 1969
Morrison, Reg, Australia - Land Beyond Time, New Holland, 2002
Nicholas, F & J, Darwin in Australia, Cambridge University Press, 2008
O'Brian, Patrick, Joseph Banks, Collins Harvill, 1987
Oosterzee, Penny van, Where Worlds Collide, Reed Books, 1997
Paul Spencer Sochaczewski, An Inordinate Fondness For Beetles, Editions Didier Millet, 2012
Quammen, David, The Song of the Dodo, Pimlico, 1996
Queiroz, Alan de, The Monkey's Voyage, Basic Books, 2014
Raby, Peter, Alfred Russel Wallace, Pimlico, 2002
Severin, Tim, The Spice Islands Voyage, Carroll and Graff, 1998

Wallace, Alfred Russel, The Malay Archipelago, Oxford University Press, 1989

Wegener, Alfred, The Origin of Continents and Oceans (Fourth Edition), Methuen, 1929

White, Mary, The Greening of Gondwana, Reed Books, 1986

Whye and Rookmaaker, Alfred Russel Wallace - Letters from the Malay Archipelago , Oxford University Press, 2013

Williams, Glyn, Naturalists at Sea, Yale University Press, 2013

Williams-Ellis, Anabel, Darwin's Moon, Blackie , 1996

Wills, C, The Darwinian Tourist, Oxford University Press, 2010

Wilson, J, The Forgotten Naturalist, Australian Scholarly Publishing, 2000

Wulf, Andrea, The Invention of Nature, John Murray, 2015

Darwin, Darwin Online, http://darwin-online.org.uk/

Wallace, Wallace Online, http://wallace-online.org/

Author Note

The publication of the book *Spice Islands* in 2011 prompted a lot of interest in Eastern Indonesia, and I was asked by many readers:

'Exactly where are the Spice Islands'?

"How do you get there"?

"How difficult is it to travel around the Spice Islands"?

"Do I need to travel backpacker style to get there"?

"Is it dangerous"?

"Are there pirates"?

In response to these questions, I decided to lead annual sailing voyages around the Spice Islands on a Bugis pinisi called the *Ombak Putih (White Wave)*, which is in part a copy of a western schooner of the mid-nineteenth century that traded around the archipelago during that period.

We sail from Ambon, and the highlight of our voyage is the visit to the Banda Islands. These islands are the only place in the world where commercial nutmegs originally grew and it is still a mystery to me as to exactly how the nutmeg tree came to these remote islands in the middle of the vast Banda Sea. As the *Ombak Putih* sails into the beautiful natural harbour of Banda Neira, an exotic scent wafts on the breeze coming from the forests of nutmeg trees that cover the islands. As we anchor opposite the town, I carefully observe the variety of tropical trees, the shapes of their leaves, and all the different shades of green covering the slopes of *Gunung Api* (Fire Mountain), which looms over the town.

After the Banda Massacre in 1621 and the elimination of almost the entire population of Banda, the Dutch East India Company (VOC) gained complete control of the islands and divided them into allotments, these were leased to Dutch planters who were obliged to sell their nutmegs to the VOC at a fixed cost. Overlooking the town is Fort Belgica, built by the VOC to protect its nutmeg monopoly, the massive stone pentagon with circular towers is still largely intact.

From Banda we sail around the north coast of Ambon Island and then through the Haruku Strait to the island of Manipa. Here we make a muddy landing ashore and trek a few kilometres up into the hills. Rising above the coastal swamps and streams, the hills are covered with coarse grass and short Melaleuca trees, which are regularly cropped to produce a dense foliage of leaves. Nearby, there is a traditional 'factory' where the crushed leaves are soaked overnight, then boiled in a huge vat over an open fire, where a simple still captures the vapour which condenses into eucalyptus oil, tea-tree oil, or *minyak kayu putih* as it is known in Indonesia. Every household in Indonesia has a small bottle of this oil which is rubbed onto the skin to relieve all sorts of bodily aches and pains. Melaleuca, with its peeling papery bark and leaves filled with aromatic oil glands are characteristically Australian, yet how did these Australian plant species get here? I asked the villagers if the Melaleuca had been introduced by the Dutch, they answered no, that the Melaleuca trees are native to these islands and that there are many more growing on the nearby and larger island of Buru.

We continue sailing north until we reach the narrow Patinti Strait, which lies between the large four-fingered island of Halmahera and a chain of offshore volcanic peaks rising directly out of the sea. This is one of the most beautiful sea voyages in all of Indonesia, and when the perfect cone of the volcano on the island of Tidore appears, it feels as though we've entered the realm of legend. Because for thousands of years, the twin islands of Ternate and Tidore were the world's only source of cloves and their location was always shrouded in myth and mystery. Ternate harbour lies on the narrow strait between the 'twin islands' and the volcanoes which dominate them. The town spreads from the harbour up to the lower slopes of Mount Gamalama, which is still active and erupted as recently as 2013. Significantly, the clove tree has buds shaped like an eucalyptus bud and is classified as part of the *Myrtacea* family, which have an Australian origin.

In 2013 some of our party participated in a ceremony at the 'Wallace House' organised by Flora and Fauna International, where there were speeches and traditional dances to honour the 100th Anniversary of the death of Alfred Russel Wallace. Located opposite the Sultan's Mosque and owned by a relative of his family, this house has the same floor plan as described by Alfred Russel Wallace in his book *The Malay Archipelago*, but its location does not match that described by Wallace. His original house has probably long since vanished, but it is important that his time in Ternate is recognised and that there is a point from where his famous 'Letter from Ternate' can be honoured.

I was already familiar with the 'Darwin story' and the 'Wallace story' but it was my observation on this voyage of the Melaleuca trees growing on Manipa Island which made me realise how important the 'Australian story' is to this fascinating part of the world, and was the beginnings of this book.

Other Books

THE TASMAN MAP - Ian Burnet
Abel Tasman, the Dutch East India Company and the first Dutch discoveries of Australia

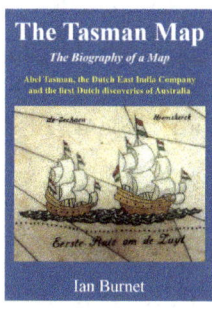

This story of the first Dutch voyages to discover Australia is set against the background of the struggle of the newly formed Dutch Republic to gain its independence from the Kingdom of Spain and the struggle of the Dutch East India Company for trade supremacy in the East Indies against its Portuguese, Spanish and English rivals.

Over a period of forty years from 1606 to 1644 and based on sixteen separate discoveries the first map of Australia took shape. The Tasman Map shows a recognisable outline of the north, west and south coasts of Australia that was not to change for another 125 years until the British explorer James Cook charted the east coast in 1770.

It was in 1933 that the Mitchell Library in Sydney acquired the Tasman Bonaparte Map. The story of how the Library managed to acquire this treasure of Dutch exploration and cartography will bring new recognition to this icon of both Dutch and Australian history,

ISBN 9780645106848 paperback A$40
ISBN 9780645106831 ebook A$20

Other Books

JOSEPH CONRAD'S EASTERN VOYAGES - Ian Burnet
  Tales of Singapore and an East Borneo River

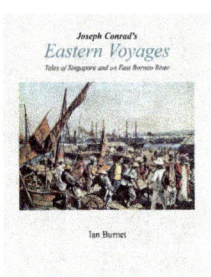

The life of Jozef Teodor Konrad Korzeniowski reads like an adventure story that could have been written by somebody like Joseph Conrad. The young Conrad became a British merchant seaman and spent fifteen years sailing on the classic three-masted, square-riggedsailing barques before they were ultimately replaced by steamships. During this period he worked his way up from able seaman, to third mate, to second mate, to first mate and finally captain of one of these beautiful ships.

Conrad loved the 'mysterious East' and his first books - *Almayer's Folly, An Outcast of the Islands, Lord Jim* and *The Rescue* were all set in Borneo and based on the people and places he encountered in his own voyages as first mate on a trading vessel based out of Singapore. In this book, Ian Burnet connects the fictional and real worlds of Conrad's life in South East Asia.

ISBN 9780645106680 0 paperback A$40
ISBN 9780645106817 ebook A$20

www.ianburnetbooks.com

Other Books

DANGEROUS PASSAGE - A Maritime History of the Torres Strait - Ian Burnet

The passage between the Australian mainland and Papua New Guinea remains the most hazardous of all the major straits in the world, and the Torres Strait Islanders have a strong seafaring tradition. This book will follow the history of the Islanders and the first sailing voyages by the Europeans who tried to make this dangerous passage. It was the voyages of these early navigators, such as Torres, Cook, Bligh, Flinders, and the British Navy hydrographers, such as King, Wickham. Blackwood, Yule and Stanley, who contributed to the charting of the Torres Strait and ultimately its use as a major shipping route.

Readers should be advised that this history will include stories of murder, mayhem, mutiny, desperate voyages of survival in open boats, headhunting and hurricanes.

ISBN 9780645106855 paperback A$40
ISBN 9780645106862 ebook A$20

www.ianburnetbooks.com

www.ingramcontent.com/pod-product-compliance
Lightning Source LLC
Chambersburg PA
CBHW051422290426
44109CB00016B/1393